Spectacular Experiments & Mad Science Kids Love

Science That Dazzles @ Home, School or On the Go!

Steve Heuer

authorHOUSE®

AuthorHouse™
1663 Liberty Drive
Bloomington, IN 47403
www.authorhouse.com
Phone: 1-800-839-8640

First published by AuthorHouse   4/26/2010

ISBN: 978-1-4490-7043-4 (e)
ISBN: 978-1-4490-7041-0 (sc)

Library of Congress Control Number: 2010903780

Printed in the United States of America
Bloomington, Indiana

This book is printed on acid-free paper.

I would like to dedicate this book to all the people who made it possible. Thank you Irina, Maddy, Sean, Ashley, Paige, Tatyana, Misha, Kristina, Gigi, Kendra, the wonderful editors at AuthorHouse, and the thousands of incredible kids who taught me how to be at my best in sharing exciting, hands-on experiments and the wonders of science!

CONTENTS

CHAPTER 1: COOLEST CHEMISTRY

Color-Changing Octopus
A classic acid-base test with a twist!

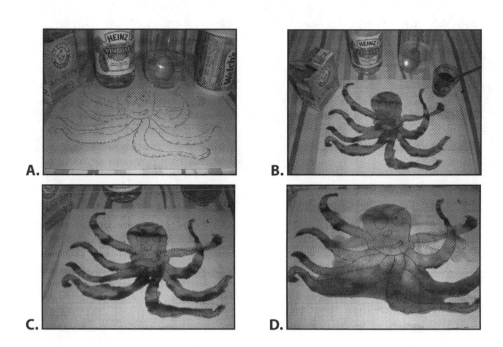

A.   B.

C.   D.

Materials:
- baking soda
- vinegar
- window cleaner
- orange juice
- a paintbrush
- grape juice
- Q-tips

What You Do:

1. Draw one to three octopi in sketch outline form only (no interior parts). (See photo A.)

2. Paint each octopus with your grape juice chemical "indicator" (it's an indicator of acids and bases). Let the grape juice dry. (See photo B.)

3. Paint the purple octopus with a base, such as baking soda or an ammonia-based window cleaner, and watch it turn blue. Photo C shows an example of the color change.

4. Next, paint with an acid, such as acetic acid (vinegar) or orange juice, and watch the octopus turn red or pink as shown in photo D.

5. Try using lemonade, nonfat milk, and other safe chemicals to test which ones are acids and which are bases. You can write your name and draw pictures in the grape juice indicator!

The Science:

All chemicals are classified as either acids or bases on the pH scale. Acids turn red and bases change color to blue or green in the presence of an indicator, such as our grape juice.

Octopi facts: These gentle bottom dwellers are some of the smartest animals in the salty seas. In order for octopi to hide from predators and prey, they change color! When attacked, octopi can flee, sting with their poison, or even shoot out ink! Amazingly, octopi are kept as pets, even though these eight-armed invertebrates can be deadly! Anyone want to arm wrestle?

H₂O Drag Race
Micro-racing fun!

Materials:

- a pipette or eye dropper
- wax paper
- white copy paper
- a marker or pencil
- a small cup of water
- a Popsicle stick

What You Do:

1. Draw a maze at least one inch wide with curved edges. Indicate start and finish points as shown in photo A.

2. Cover the maze with a sheet of wax paper and tape it down. (See photo B.)

3. Squeeze a drop of water onto the starting line as illustrated in photo C.

4. Look at photo D, then grab a Popsicle stick and "drag" race the water drop to the finish line! Race against the clock or a friend!

The Science:

Water molecules bond together with other substances, such as the wooden "drag race" stick. However, H₂O does not stick to wax paper very well, providing an ideal, friction-free racetrack for your water molecules.

Mad Science Potion
The ultimate chemistry concoction!

Materials
- small bottles
- A few ounces each of iodine and liquid starch
- vitamin C tablets
- 1 tablespoon of baking soda
- 1/2 cup of vinegar
- 1 tablet of food coloring
- a large, clear glass pitcher filled two-thirds of the way with clean water
- safety gloves and goggles
- a spoon

What You Do:

1. Start with a tall pitcher filled close to the top with water.

2. Add two tablespoons of liquid starch and stir for two minutes until water is nearly clear.

3. Measure and pour in two tablespoons of iodine. The "potion" becomes purple or blue.

4. Now, say the magic words, "Chemistry is like magic!" as you secretly drop in two vitamin C tablets. Stir them into the large pitcher! The water becomes clear again!

5. Now, for the grand finale, drop in one tablespoon of baking soda and a food color tablet, quickly followed by the vinegar! A potion eruption!

The Science:

Iodine turns blue in the presence of a starch. When added, the vitamin C consumes the iodine, thus removing the element and returning the water/starch mixture to its original clarity. The addition of baking soda and vinegar creates a grand finale reaction to your mad science potion: the acid and base react to create a tsunami of bubbles!

Tic-Toc Reaction

Time is on your side!

Materials:

- ½ gallon of purified water
- two large glass bottles (fruit jars are good)
- five 1000-milligram or greater tablets of vitamin C
- a small bottle of iodine (available at most grocery stores or pharmacies)
- hydrogen peroxide
- liquid laundry starch

Preparation:

Crush your five vitamin C (ascorbic acid) tablets and mix the powder into five to seven ounces of very warm water. You may want to label this glass "Vitamin C Solution."

What You Do:

1. In one of your large glass bottles, add seven ounces of water to seven teaspoons of hydrogen peroxide and two teaspoons of liquid starch solution. Label this "Solution A."

2. Prepare your second large bottle by adding three teaspoons of iodine into seven ounces of your vitamin C solution. Label this "Solution B."

3. Pour Solution A into Solution B. Place the bottles down so you can watch the amazing reaction: a deep, dark blue appears from nowhere!

The Science:

This one involves two chemical reactions! The iodine and hydrogen peroxide mixture turns blue because starch is present. However, this does not occur right away, as the vitamin C quickly consumes the iodine. Eventually, the vitamin C gets used up, and hydrogen peroxide and iodine are still present, so they turn deep blue in color since starch is present!

Sands of Jupiter

Create reusable sculptures from your homemade science sand!

Materials:

- 6 cups of clean playground sand, purchased at a toy store
- 3 cups of cornstarch
- 1 1/2 cups of water
- 1 cup of mineral oil
- a large bowl
- food coloring

What You Do:

1. Pour the six cups of clean sand into the large bowl.

2. Slowly mix in the cornstarch.

3. Add ten drops of food coloring to the mixture.

4. Add the whole cup of mineral oil and mix it in thoroughly for a full five minutes. (If the mixture is too moist after mixing, add another half cup of sand. If it's too dry, add another quarter cup of mineral oil.)

5. Mold, experiment, and play with your new space sand!

6. When not in use, store the sand in an airtight container and place it in a cool area.

The Science:

The cornstarch together with a liquid makes a colloid, which is a hybrid between a solid and a liquid, giving the moist sand its solid yet fluid behavior!

Super Ooze!
World's best slime formula!

Materials:

- about 12 ounces of *clear* Elmer's Glue (has a slight blue tint)
- a box of Borax laundry booster
- a strong plastic bowl
- a plastic spoon
- a few drops of food coloring

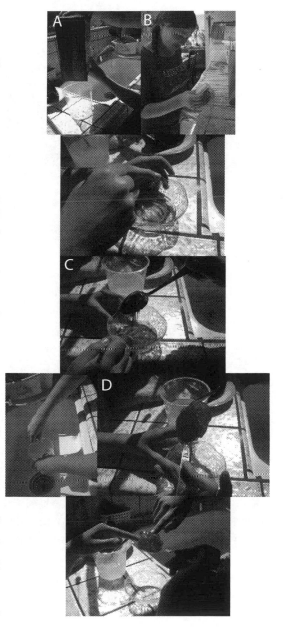

What You Do:

1. Dissolve one tablespoon of Borax powder into a glass with seven to ten ounces of hot water and mix for five minutes until mostly dissolved. (See photo A.)

2. Pour all the glue into the plastic bowl as indicated in photo B.

3. Add four to five drops of food coloring into the bowl of glue and gently stir until evenly mixed.

4. Now add about an ounce of Borax solution (dissolved Borax and water) into the colored glue and begin mixing.

5. After two minutes of mixing in the first ounce of the solution. add another tablespoon of Borax solution.

6. If the "super ooze" is too dry, add about an ounce of additional clear glue. If the mixture is too moist and is not forming into a uniform plastic bouncing putty, add another ounce of Borax solution. (See photo C.)

7. Next, once the ooze has formed into what resembles something like a bouncing putty, place the ooze in your hands. You can squeeze it, roll it, and form the putty into your super bouncing ooze as illustrated in photo D.

8. You may bounce your new polymer creation. You can stretch it, toss it, or even stick a straw into it and blow bubbles. You can add some zinc sulfide to make it glow in the dark. Be sure to keep it fresh by placing it in a Ziploc bag when not in use.

The Science:

You have created a plastic polymer with repeating, linked molecules. The mineral-based Borax helps it all come together.

Special Effects Blood

Anyone want to star in their own horror film?

 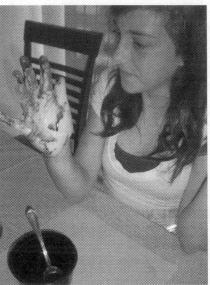

Materials:
- 1 quart of clear corn syrup
- a bottle of red food coloring
- 2 drops of blue food coloring
- 1/2 cup of Rose's grenadine
- a empty, clean plastic fruit jar
- a metal spoon

What You Do:

Simply mix all the ingredients. The special effects blood should be nice and red, and it should drip slowly. Get your friends together and make your horror film or play!

The Science:

The combination of chemicals helps create a thickness similar to actual blood. Human blood has four main parts. Red blood cells move oxygen throughout the body. White blood cells fight infections. Platelets create scabs to help healing. Plasma, which is mostly made out of water, allows other parts of blood to travel through the body.

Big-Time Volcano

Launch "the big one" from your backyard!

Materials and Preparation:
- an empty two-liter bottle filled one-third of the way full of water
- 1 quart of vinegar
- a small box of baking soda
- a squirt of Dawn dish soap
- food coloring
- a funnel
- empty plastic cups or plastic containers
- a camera—you just don't want to miss this!
- a place you can perform this erupting experiment that won't harm Mom's flower bed!

What You Do:

1. Using the funnel, pour the quart of vinegar into the bottle.

2. Add a few drops of Dawn dish soap and food coloring.

3. Pour three to four tablespoons of baking soda into two cups of very warm water. Mix the solution until the baking soda is dissolved.

3. Now, pour your cups of vinegar from about two feet above the opening of your soda bottle. You should get a one- to four-foot-high volcanic eruption!

The Science:

The acid (vinegar) and base (baking soda) reacted, causing an eruption of carbon dioxide, soap, and coloring. The reaction is safe even as the gas bubbles flow all over! (In the event the volcanic eruption covers you, simply wash your clothes in cold water to remove all the chemicals safely!)

Milk Fireworks
A rainbow of "flowering" colors!

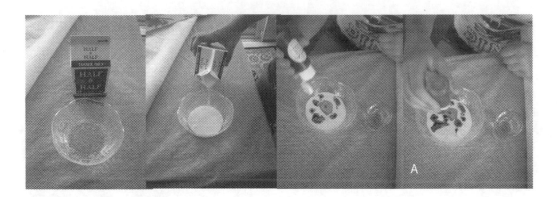

Materials:
- prepare a bowl of regular milk
- a pipette or eye dropper
- four or more different food colorings
- a small cup of dish soap, such as Dawn
- ten cotton Q-tips

What You Do:

1. Drop ten to twenty drops of various food colors into the bowl of milk. **Do not** spread the drops. (See photo A.)

2. Dip one end of a Q-tip into your dish soap and immediately press that soapy end into one of the drops of food coloring. Quickly remove it. (See photo B.)

3. Continue dipping Q-tips that have been dipped in soap into the various color spots of the food coloring. **Never mix**, just dip and remove each time! (See photo C.)

4. The tie-dye effect will continue for about ten minutes, so be sure to keep observing.

The Science:

Milk contains fat and nonfat components. When you added the dish soap, the fat was separated from the nonfat part of the milk. As the fat part of the milk moved, it carried the food coloring along, creating the colorful fireworks effect. Also, the chemicals in the dish soap can break the "bonds" of the nonfat molecules, creating additional firework effects.

Five-Minute Tie-dye
A great and low-cost tie-dye experiment

Materials:
- a bottle of rubbing alcohol
- several Sharpie or other quality permanent markers
- a pipette or eye dropper
- a plain, white T-shirt or square of white cloth
- a round bowl
- a rubber band

What You Do:

1. Lay out your white T-shirt in a clean area.

2. Decorate the middle or any other part of the shirt you would like to have tie-dyed. Using your markers, write your name or draw shapes, pictures, etc. (See photo A.)

3. Using your eye dropper or pipette, drip alcohol onto various points of your artwork. (See photo B.)

4. Watch as the pens bleed into one another, creating a tie-dye effect as shown in photo C.

The Science:

The Sharpie ink does not react in water, but it is soluble in rubbing alcohol. The alcohol carries the ink molecules after it breaks their chemical bonds. You may notice colors inside of colors—i.e., black ink will separate into many colors, including brown, blue, and red.

Oxygen Volcano
Observe this fast-moving chemical reaction!

Materials and Preparation:
- one 12- to 16-ounce plastic or glass soda bottle with a narrow neck
- food coloring
- a bottle of regular hydrogen peroxide
- 1/2 ounce of Dawn or Joy dish soap
- 1 to 2 teaspoons of yeast dissolved in 1/4 cup of very warm water
- a foil pie pan
- a funnel

What You Do:

1. Pour half a cup of hydrogen peroxide into a bottle. (See photo A.)

2. Add five drops of food coloring. Then, add the dish soap.

3. Pour the yeast mixture into the bottle quickly and remove the funnel as shown in photo B. Watch the foam of soap, oxygen bubbles, and water erupt!

The Science:

This exothermic (heated) reaction occurs when the yeast speeds up the release of oxygen molecules within the hydrogen peroxide (H_2O_2) molecules. Once one oxygen molecule is released, the H_2O_2 molecule simply becomes H_2O: water!

Titan's Wave in a Bottle

A hands-on, portable "wave maker" that's perfect for your room!

Materials:
- a clean, empty two-liter bottle
- 2 cups of mineral or baby oil
- 10 drops of blue or green food coloring
- a funnel

What You Do:

1. Fill the bottle two-thirds of the way full of clean, clear water as illustrated in photo A.

2. Add ten drops of blue food coloring. (See photo B.)

3. Funnel mineral or baby oil into the bottle until it is just short of overfilling. (See photo C.) Close the bottle top tightly.

4. Now, holding the bottle on its side as shown in photo D, give it a gentle back-and-forth shaking movement, like the motion of a wave!

The Science:

The oil is less heavy than the water and will flow like a wave above the blue water! Shake the bottle fiercely and watch as the immiscible liquids spread, yet settle back, reforming the wave in a bottle!

Lava Lamp to Go

Create a lava effect in just a few minutes!

Materials and Preparation:
- a clean, empty two-liter bottle
- water
- food coloring
- 2 cups of cooking oil
- 2 tablets of Alka-Seltzer broken into quarters (eight pieces in all)
- a funnel

What You Do:

1. Fill the bottle two-thirds of the way full of water.

2. Add a few drops of food coloring. (See photo A.)

3. Add two cups of cooking oil. (See photo B.)

4. Now add one of the quarter pieces of Alka-Seltzer (see photo C) into the bottle of chemicals and watch!

5. Continue adding the Alka-Seltzer quarter-tablets every few minutes to continue the "lava lamp" effect!

You can keep the lava lamp in your room and add more Alka-Seltzer tablets anytime you want!

The Science:

Initially, the oil floats on top of the water because it is less dense than the water. When added, the heavier Alka-Seltzer sinks to the bottom, carrying the oil along with it. As the tablets dissolve, bubbles are created. The gas bubbles/oil mixture rises because the bubbles are lighter then the water, creating the lava lamp effect!

CHAPTER 2: MAD LAB

Vampire Stakes
Garlic is not the only way to fend off a vampire!

Materials:
- gallon-sized or XXL-sized Ziploc bags with zippers
- 10 to 20 colorful sharpened pencils or skewers
- water
- food coloring
- permanent markers

What You Do:

1. Draw a picture of a vampire or monster or your own creation on the face of one side of your extra-large Ziploc bag.

2. Fill your large bag two-thirds of the way full of water.

3. Add five to seven drops of food coloring. Zip your bag closed.

4. Start piercing into the bag by screwing the pencils through, under the water level as shown. Your piercing movement should be straight and quick so you do not create too large of a hole or any leaks.

The Science:

The Ziploc bag is made of a plastic formed of polymers (chained together, repeating molecules). The polymers hold onto each other very strongly. Together with the power of air pressure and water tension (the water molecules' bond), you are able to pierce a Ziploc bag with multiple vampire stakes without it leaking! You may display this in your room!

Vampire Stakes, Jr.
A handy-sized version of "Vampire Stakes."

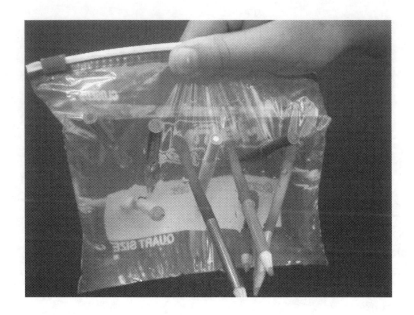

Materials:
- quart-sized Ziploc bags with zippers
- water
- pencils
- broad-stroke permanent markers
- food coloring (optional)

What You Do:

1. On the Ziploc bag, draw a picture of a vampire or any other monster boldly with your colorful, broad-stroke permanent markers.

2. Fill your Ziploc bag about two-thirds of the way full of clean tap water. Add a few drops of food coloring if you choose.

3. Zip the bag closed.

4. Start piercing your Ziploc bag by screwing in your pencils, pushing them straight through to the other side without hesitation.

5. The pencils will remain lodged in both sides.

6. Now see how many pencils you can add!

7. When you are done, remove the pencils quickly for a waterfall effect!

The Science:

Ziplocs bags are made of a strong polymer plastic that holds together very well. Also, air pressure is pushing from all sides. This helps keep the water from leaking through the holes where the stakes are above the water line.. Finally, water molecules love to hold onto other water molecules; we call this water tension or water adhesion!

Super-Sized Monster Straw

Where did my Icee go?

Materials:

• five to ten colorful Icee-brand straws, available at your local 7-11 convenience store

• a beverage of your choice

What You Do:

Icee brand straws from 7-11 have a special wedge-like opening on one end that connects well with the regular-shaped hole opening on the other end of another straw. Start by connecting two straws together and try drinking through the both of them. Now, add five to ten additional straws to create a monster-sized straw and place the end into your beverage. Start sucking. What happened to your liquid?

The Science:

Drinking with one straw is easy, as there is very little air pressure inside the straw to compete with as you suck up your drink. When you add many more straws, you have much more air space inside the straws and therefore air pressure pushing against the pressure you are creating on the other end! Who will win the sipping and air-pressure contest?

Activity Zone!

*Try sipping with 10 straws connected.

*Have everyone connect five straws each and have a sipping contest! First one finished wins!

* Make holes in your connected straws and try drinking!

Bloody Handprint
Not for the faint of heart!

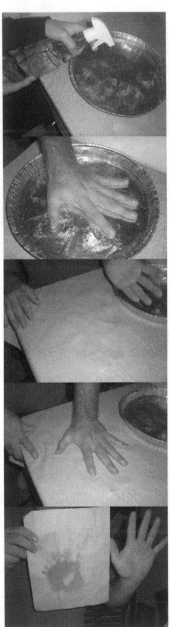

Materials and Preparation:
- chemically treated Goldenrod Paper, available at a teacher learning store or online
- 2 tablespoons baking soda, dissolved in a cup of water
- a bottle of window cleaner with ammonia
- a cup of orange juice
- a cup of vinegar
- a paintbrush
- Q-tips

What You Do:

Before starting, you may want to check out the video of this experiment on www.SteveSpanglerScience.com.

1. Using a paintbrush, start painting on your Goldenrod Paper with the baking soda solution (a base) or window cleaner (an acid).

2. Next, paint over your baking soda (base) solution with lemon juice, orange juice, or vinegar.

3. As a grand finale, get a second sheet of Goldenrod Paper, dip your hand directly into a bowl of window cleaner, and press down onto the clean sheet.

4. Quickly remove your hand from the "bloody handprint just made visible on the magic color-changing paper!

The Science:

The chemically treated Goldenrod Paper is coated with a weak acid. Adding a base will cause the paper to react and turn red!

Supersized Screaming Balloons
The balloon will not be the only one screaming with delight!

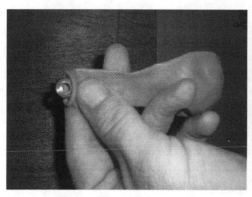 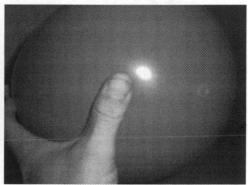

Materials:

- strong, colorful latex balloons 18 inches or larger—the bigger, the more dramatic
- small hex nuts

What You Do:

1. Drop one hex nut into an uninflated latex balloon
2. Holding the hex nut through the balloon as shown, blow up the balloon about 75 percent full of air.
3. Tie the balloon closed.
4. Grasp the balloon firmly and begin moving the balloon in a circle.
5. Listen to the sound!

The Science:

The friction of the metal hex nut rubbing against the balloon creates a shrieking sound due to the vibrations of the hex nut rubbing against the balloon! *Be careful*: the friction can cause the balloon to pop.

Alien Balloons
An alien invasion in your living room!

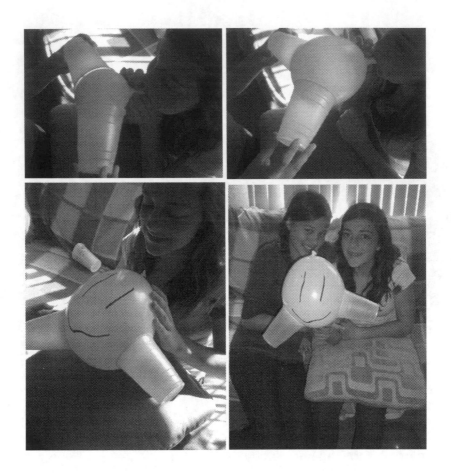

Materials:
- colorful permanent or washable markers
- several 12-inch or larger balloons
- strong, medium-sized plastic white or clear cups
- friends

What You Do:

1. Decorate your white cups with any "alien" design you choose.

2. Draw an alien face on your balloon with various colorful markers.

3. Stretch out your balloon and begin blowing in up until it is about one-third full of air.

4. Now get two or three friends to help you. Continue blowing up the balloon as your friends press several cups against it. With a little practice, the cups should stick against the balloon as shown! Try using the cups as antennae!

The Science:

Air pressure is exerting its force at all times in all directions. The gasses trapped inside the cup exert pressure, as does the outside air pressure, holding the cups onto the balloon.

Go Extreme: Giant Alien Balloon Blow-Up!

Follow the same procedure above, but use larger, thirty-six-inch balloons instead of smaller ones!

Orbs Arising!

Warning! Raise 'em only in a "mad lab."

Materials:

- Obtain these amazing little plastic orbs at a science or hobby store.

What You Do:

Simply place the polymer, water-absorbing orbs in a container of water and over time they will expand to over two hundred times their original size!

The Science:

These water-absorbent polymers (linked, repeating molecules of plastic) grow as water penetrates the solid orbs!

Activity Zone!

*Try adding water, soda or other safe beverages on top of a few dry orbs.

* Place your hydrated orbs in the sun for a full day!

* Place your hydrated orbs in the refrigerator and/or freezer and observe after a few hours.

* Bounce them! Catch them! Perform your own safe experiments!

Creature Feature

You may want to sleep with one eye open!

Materials and Preparation:
- Your local dollar store will usually carry these plastic 'grow creatures".

What You Do:

Simply place your "grow creatures" in water and watch them expand to enormous sizes!

Activity Zone!

*Place your expanded creatures out in the sun for a full day!

*Raise a colony of "alien" creatures in a two or three liter bottle filled with water!

*Place one of your "dry" creatures in a small container full of water and set the container in the freezer. In a few hours, observe and record the results.

The Science:

These super-absorbing polymer plastics can hold their shape as they grow two hundred times their initial size!

Sound Whip
Create a sound sensation in your neighborhood!

Materials and Preparation:
- 10 to 15 feet of corrugated plastic drainage tube, available at your local hardware or home improvement store. The tube should have a diameter as little as possible; 3 to 5 inches is ideal!

What You Do:

With adult supervision, spray paint your "sound whips," if you like. Swing your lightweight tube in a circular motion over your head. The faster you swing, the louder the sound!

The Science:

The shrieking sound waves are created when the "excited" molecules in the air quickly escape through the tube's narrow opening. (The inspiration for this science demonstration is Steve Spangler's published experiment, "Whirly—The Twirling Sound Hose." Watch a video of this on www.SteveSpanglerScience.com!)

Sound Barrier Breaker
Travel faster than the speed of sound!

Materials:

- a long leather belt

What You Do:

Try flicking the belt outward, using your wrist to pull back on it just as the belt reaches full extension A second method is to fold your belt in half and grab the two newly created rounded ends as shown. Push the middle area inward to create a bulge, and then pull back on the rounded ends very quickly!

The Science:

Did you hear that cracking sound? Then you just broke the sound barrier: about 770 miles per hour! Experiment with different angles, being sure to use your wrist to pull back on your belt at as it reaches its end!

Fifty Foot- Mobile Phone
Have you tried the latest model?

Materials:
- four 10 to 15 foot corrugated plastic drainage tubes, available at your local hardware or home improvement store
- duct tape
- spray paint (optional)

What You Do:

Tape each piece of tubing end to end with duct tape. Spray paint the tube with your own designs to customize your "mobile phone." Grab a friend and start talking!

Tips: Experiment with talking around corners or from several feet away from the tubes.

The Science:

Sound is the movement of vibrating waves and requires the atmosphere's gasses to travel. Since space is condensed inside the "mobile phone," many of those vibrating waves reach our ears when the air molecules quickly escape the opening of the tubes! Texting not available!

Snowballs In Summer
And fall, spring, and winter!

Materials:
- a bottle of plastic "snow" powder, manufactured by Insta-Snow.

What You Do:

Follow the instructions on the bottle to create a realistic-looking artificial snow. Pour a full bottle of the snow powder on your front lawn, and then pour a few buckets full of water over the substance. Snow in the summer, fall, and spring—and it's biodegradable! This snow makes for great snowball fights, mini-snowman building, and much more! When you are finished experimenting, gather the snow up, put it in a bucket, and place the bucket in the sun! The snow will return to its original powder to be reused over and over again!

The Science:

The plastic powder, which is made in a laboratory, absorbs and holds water extremely well. The powder is even used at ski resorts when Mother Nature does not provide enough snow on her own! Of course, you can attempt this experiment during all four seasons!

Secret Message Magic

Science + secrets = hands-on fun!

Materials:
- a travel-sized bottle of Tide liquid laundry soap
- three or four sheets of colorful card stock paper
- a few regular small-head bristle paintbrushes
- a portable black light
- an empty cup for paint

What You Do:

With the lights on, lightly paint your secret message onto a sheet of colored card stock paper using Tide liquid soap. Turn the lights off, aim the black light toward your message, and let the magic begin!

The Science:

Liquid Tide contains a fluorescent chemical that is activated by the ultraviolet rays produced by a black light. The fluorescent chemical in the liquid Tide then changes the ultraviolet light into visible light. Try adding liquid Tide to bubble solution to make ultraviolet bubbles that glow under a black light!

Extreme Danger: DO NOT OPEN
Get ready to laugh

Materials:
- a clean, empty two-liter soda bottle
- a small nail
- a water faucet
- a sharpie (black is good!)
- food coloring (red is good!)

What You Do:

1. Make about eight to ten small holes around the middle and lower third of the empty bottle, the holes at least two inches apart from each other.

2. Fill the bottle completely to the top, adding a few drops of red or blue food coloring to resemble some kind of poison or potion! You will notice water leaking out of the holes in small streams. Don't worry, this is normal.

3. When the bottle is totally full of the colored water, screw on the bottle top. Your leaks will stop!

4. Next, write on the bottle the ominous words: "Extreme Danger! **Do not open!** A very curious passerby will get soaked when he fails to heed these words!

The Science:

Air is constantly exerting its pressure from all sides, which is what causes the water to stream out from the bottle. When you tighten the lid on the top, the air pressure around the bottle starts keeping the water from streaming out!

Soap Cloud

Get your camera ready!

Materials:

- several brands of bar soap, including Dove
- a microwave oven
- paper towels
- a bucket three-quarters of the way full of water

What You Do:

1. Drop all the bars of soap into the water. Only Dove and Ivory brand soaps float! (Bars of these brands are filled with air, so they are less dense than the water they float upon.)

2. Next, place a few layers of paper towels in the microwave.

3. Place one Dove bar of soap in the middle of the microwave on the layer of paper towels.

4. Close the microwave and set it on high power for five minutes. Keep an eye on the soap through the microwave door. You will be amazed as you watch a billowing white cloud of soap expand and fill the microwave!

5. When the time expires, quickly remove the heated, layered cloud and place it on a plate. Touch and examine the soap as it begins to slowly deflate!

The Science:

A bar of Dove soap contains air. The heat from the microwave expands the gasses contained inside the soap, causing Dove bar to expand and billow into a white cloud! When the soap is removed from the microwave, the soap cools and therefore begins to shrink as the air contracts.

Go Extreme: The Blob/Super Ooze 2
Keep the lights on at night!

Materials:
- a large, durable plastic container
- 1 gallon or more of clear glue
- a box of Borax soap
- a bottle of food coloring
- 3 to 4 gallons of water in a bucket of very warm water
- your two hands
- a large wooden mixing spoon
- zinc sulfide (optional) for a glow-in-the-dark effect

What You Do:

1. Pour all the clear gel glue into your plastic container.

2. Pour four cups of Borax powder into your bucket of very warm water.

3. Mix the Borax for ten minutes with a wooden stirrer.

4. Squeeze twenty drops of food coloring into the bucket and mix for thirty seconds.

5. Pour all your Borax solution (water, Borax, and food coloring) into the plastic container holding the glue.

6. Now, use your hands to mix in all the chemicals. Twenty to thirty minutes later, you should have your own personal pet blob!

The Science:

You have mixed together chemicals to make a polymer plastic blob you can bounce, stretch, and blow into giant bubbles or even use as a prop for your latest horror movie! Add a few teaspoons of water daily to keep it moist. It should last for about a month if sealed in an extra large Ziploc bag!

Tip: you may rip off a small handful of your blob to use to blow bubbles with a straw. You can add zinc sulfide to make your blob glow in the dark. You can also bounce your blob, stretch it, place it overnight in the freezer. The possibilities are endless. Anyone want to make a monster movie?

Pinhole Camera Grocery Bag
Upside down vision!

Materials:
- a large, clear plastic grocery bag
- black card stock paper or poster board that you cannot see through
- scissors
- tape

What You Do:

1. Draw one big circle on each side of the bag.

2. Draw one smaller circle, on the outside of the bag, inside one of the two larger circles.

3. Cut out a black circle of card stock paper and tape it, inside the bag, so it's covering the large circle where you also have your small circle on the outside of the bag. Make sure the black circle fully covers the large circle. (See photo A.)

4. Push a sharpened pencil through both the black paper and the tiny hole as shown in photo B. Do not make this hole bigger than the little circle you drew.

5. Turn the bag around, open it up, and look through the hole you did not cover with black paper.

6. Look at any object in bright sunlight from your large hole. Is the world upside down?

The Science:

Light travels in straight lines. Yet, when it passes through a tiny hole, the image gets flipped. This is why a camera has a small mirror inside, to flip the inside right side up. Your eye also receives images upside down when light enters your pupil. The brain flips the image right side up so you may go about your daily life in a normal way!

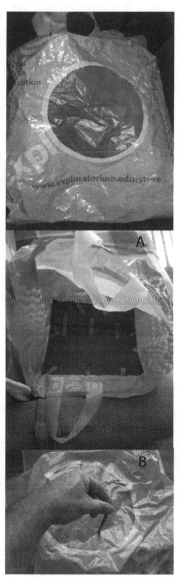

Kid-Created Kaleidoscope
The "beauty" of recycling!

Materials and Preparation:

- a clear tennis ball can
- a sheet of transparent plastic, available at a print store
- three 2 ¼-inch by 7 ½-inch long cut glass strips with opaque backing, such as cardboard, which you can get from a local mirror store
- masking tape
- shiny and colorful objects such as confetti and plastic jewels
- stickers and/or permanent markers

What You Do:

1. Form a triangular "prism" with the mirrored sides positioned inward.

2. Tape the three mirrors together from the outside with masking tape.

3. Cut a hole in the plastic cap of the tennis ball container.

4. Cut a small square out of the plastic sheet that is a little larger than the hole you have in the cap.

5. Tape this square over the hole on the inside of the cap.

6. Next, cut out a circle of clear plastic with a diameter of two and seven-eighths inches.

7. Now place your parts together from bottom to top. Add your colorful and shiny objects and place at the bottom of your tennis can. Next, place your large plastic circle on top of your objects. Now, carefully place your mirrored triangular prism on top of your plastic circle kaleidoscope. Finally, simply put on your lid! Decorate the kaleidoscope with stickers or markers if you wish!

The Science:

Light bounces off the mirrors and the beautiful objects to create a dazzling art and science project! Of course, light is critical in creating your visible lightshow! The mirrors give the illusion that your objects have doubled in quantity!

Periscope Up!

A real, working periscope in less than an hour!

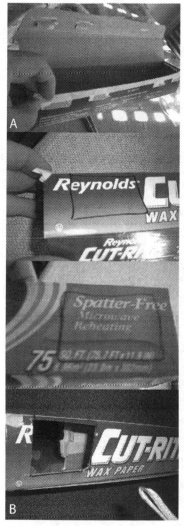

Materials:

- one empty plastic wrap or aluminum foil box
- masking tape
- two small 2-inch by 3-inch mirrors
- scissors

What You Do:

1. Completely cover the sharp cutting edge of the aluminum foil box with masking tape as shown in photo A.

2. Cut a rectangular hole near the bottom of the front side of the box about one and one-half inches long and one inch wide. (See photo B.)

3. Cut another hole the same size at the back of the opposite end of the box as shown in photo C.

4. Tape the mirrors at an angle of about forty-five degrees with the reflecting sides both facing toward one another as shown.

5. Look into the bottom mirror. You should be able to see above you through the top mirror, just as a periscope on a submarine sees above water! (See photo D.)

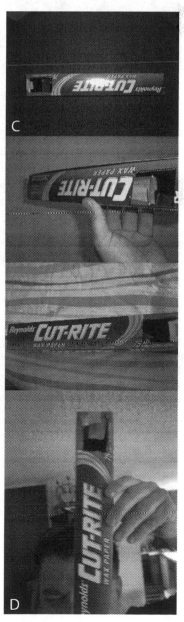

The Science:

The mirrors help redirect your view so you can see above your normal line of sight! Light enters the periscope and bounces off the mirrors!

Go Extreme: "Night Vision?"

At night with the lights on, take note of the objects surrounding you and their colors. Gradually darken the room, but leave enough light so you can still see the objects. Where have all the colors gone?

The Science:

Light is a key element in allowing us to see colors. Parts of your eye, called cones, detect colors. Other parts of your eye, called rods, allow you see black and white.

Kid-Sized Dome Home
Build and rebuild your dream home!

Materials:
- garden stakes (or plastic tubing)
- masking tape
- sturdy ground

What You Do:

Cover any sharp points of the garden stakes with masking tape to prevent injuries. Use masking tape to join the stakes together in building 3-D shapes and structures. Try creating triangles, squares, and rectangles from your stakes.Simulate an earthquake to see if your structure is sound. Take photos of your super tall tower or your human habitat. Cover your structure with bedsheets or lightweight blankets in making your stake structure a kid-sized habitat!

The Science:

Structures are formed by joining beams or other support materials. Triangles, squares and rectangles are among the strongest shapes. Precise mathematical measurements and angles work hand-in-hand with science in creating structurally sound buildings.

Balloon Bed

Experience the bed of nails phenomenon with the safety and fun of balloons!

Materials and Preparation:
- a strong, sturdy, rectangular shipping box at least 3 feet wide and 5 to 7 feet long
- about fifteen large balloons inflated with air to about 80 percent of capacity

What You Do:

Securely place the blown-up balloons into your cardboard "bed' so they do not slip out. You may want to tape them down. (You can also place several balloons into XXL-sized Ziploc bags designed to hold clothing. Zip up several balloons inside the extra large Ziplocs, place in your box and carefully lay down on your balloon bed!). Have a friend help you lie carefully across your bed of balloons, making sure your entire body comes to rest on the balloon bed at the same time. Stay perfectly still. How long until you pop a balloon?

The Science:

Like a bed of nails, your balloons support and share your distributed weight, preventing the nails from popping them.

Go Extreme: "Steel Eggs?"

Grab a raw egg out of your refrigerator. Squeeze it as strongly as you can in the palm of one hand without using your thumb. Is it hard to break? The egg's shape redistributes the force of your hand's squeeze.

CHAPTER 3: MOTION MANIA

Jelly Belly on Elbow
You vs. gravity!

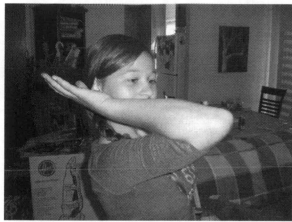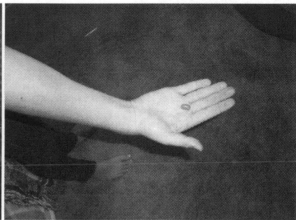

Materials:
- Jelly Belly candies
- your elbow

What You Do:

1. Balance a Jelly Belly on the forearm side of your elbow with your outstretched hand pointed up toward the sky as shown.

2. Quickly swing your arm in a circular motion toward the Jelly Belly, catching it before it starts falling to the ground!

The Science:

Newton's Law of Inertia states that an object at rest stays at rest until a force acts upon that object. The Jelly Belly will remain at rest for about half a second before gravity wins! Can you snatch that Jelly Belly in less than half a second? Keep practicing and you soon will be able to do it!

Balanced Butterfly

Find the center of gravity via a beautiful butterfly!

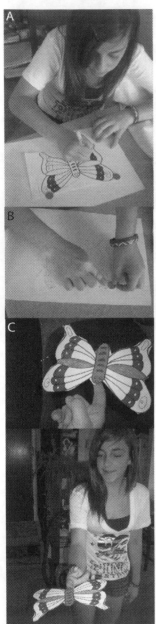

Materials:

- an outline of a beautiful butterfly on white card stock paper
- markers or crayons
- scissors
- clear tape
- pennies

What You Do:

1. Color in your butterfly as shown in photo A.

2. Cut out the insect.

3. Tape two pennies on the back side of your butterfly as shown in photo B.

4. Balance the mouth of the butterfly on your pointer finger. Move your finger up and down to get wings to flap! (See photo C.)

The Science:

You have found the butterfly's center of gravity when it is balanced on your finger!

Kissing Balloons
May make you blush!

Materials:
- two large, colorful balloons
- permanent markers
- two strings about 18 inches long each

What You Do:

1. Blow up each balloon to about 90 percent capacity and tie each closed. Draw on each balloon a picture of an alien, a monster, a best friend, or any other creative face you can think of.

2. Hold the balloons by their strings so they face one another and are about two feet apart. The balloons should remain perfectly still.

3. Take a deep breath and blow strong and steady between the balloons!

The Science:

We expect the balloons to be pushed farther apart by the current of air we create. Yet the rushing

wind creates a "vacuum," via Bernoulli's Principle, as higher-pressured air pushes out the lower-pressured air that you blew between your balloons. This movement of air pushes the balloons together.

Water Balloon Mayhem
You're going to get wet!

Materials:

- several water balloons
- a device to fill the balloon with water
- water
- friends

What You Do:

1. You and your friends each fill your balloons with water to about 80 percent of capacity.

2. Without tying them closed or spilling the water, have everyone twist the openings of their balloons about fifty times or so.

3. Making sure not to let them unwind, have everyone toss their balloons, and watch the zigzag action!

The Science:

As the balloon's neck unwraps, the action of the water exiting the balloon will cause a reaction. The changing direction of the water will cause the chaotic motion of the balloon, which is also affected by the laws of aerodynamics.

H$_2$0 Yoyo Balloon
A toy and science project all in one!

Materials & Preparation:
- one small water balloon
- one large rubber band (at least one-half an inch thick), cut so there is no longer a loop
- a device to fill the balloon with water
- water

What You Do:

1. Fill the balloon with about one cup of water.

2. Then, blow it up with air to about 80 percent of capacity.

3. Tie off the end.

4. Tie the thick rubber band to the tied end of balloon. Launch it back and forth and up and down!

The Science:

The elastic rubber band provides the potential and real energy you need to create the back-and-forth motion of a yo-yo. By adding air to your water balloon you have a more durable toy that should last long after a regular water balloon would have broken under the same conditions.

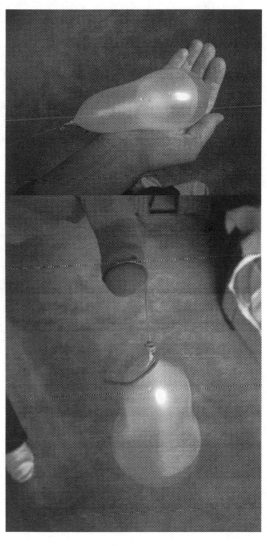

Zigzag Ball-loon

Can you catch this one?

Materials:

- the largest balloon you can find at your local party supply store
- one 3- to 4-inch-diameter soft rubber ball

What You Do:

Push the rubber ball into the mouth of the balloon. Hold the rubber ball as you blow up your balloon 90 percent full of air. Try tossing it with a friend. The ball should move rather strangely.

The Science:

While objects in motion remain in motion, the addition of the small rubber ball's weight affects the path of the balloon, as do gravity and friction.

Giant Balloon Orbit

How long can you keep your coin orbiting?

Materials:
- the largest balloon you can find at your local party supply store
- a penny or nickel

What You Do:

Simply drop the coin into a balloon. Holding the penny at the bottom of the balloon, blow up the balloon to about 75 percent capacity and tie it off. Spin the balloon quickly with your wrist and hand, causing the coin inside the balloon to orbit. Now, allow the balloon to rest in the palm of your hand. The coin should remain in orbit for several seconds!

The Science:

According to one of Newton's Laws, objects in motion remain in motion until a greater force effects that object. The coin remains in motion until the friction caused by the balloon and the gravity pulling the coin down bring the coin to a stop.

Soda 360

What comes around, goes around.

Materials and Preparation:

1. Prepare a strong, 7-inch-square piece of cardboard by taping four strings to the corners.

2. Cut four lengths of string about 20 inches long each.

3. Gather the other ends of the strings together and hold to keep the cardboard balanced.

4. Fill a two-liter bottle half full of water and add a few drops of food coloring if desired.

What You Do:

Place the two-liter bottle in the middle of your homemade contraption. Holding your arm straight and firm, swing it 360 degrees around in an orbital path. The liquid and the bottle should remain in place without a drop of liquid lost!

The Science:

The inward push toward the center while "looping" is called centripetal force, which keeps the bottle and water in place and overcomes the force of gravity.

Try adding a few cups of vinegar to the bottle and drop in one cup of baking soda just a moment before swinging to create a 360-degree volcano!

Newton's Coin

You won't believe your eyes!

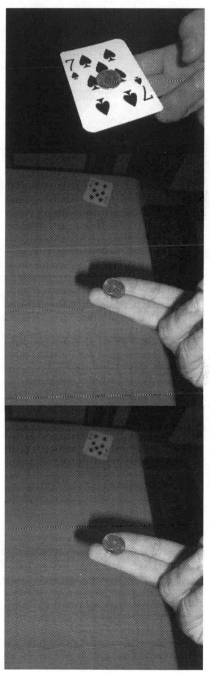

Materials:

- a coin
- a playing card

What You Do:

Challenge your friend to balance the coin on the card as shown.

Now, see if he or she can flick the card in a way that the coin remains on his or her finger while the card rockets away!

The Secret and the Science:

Hit the card straight on (not from an angled, up or down). According to Newton's Law of Inertia, objects in motion (the card) remain in motion, and objects at rest (the coin) remain at rest unless a force acts upon that object.

With practice, you will master this experiment!

Newton's Apple Tower'

Give mom a good warning before trying this one!

Materials:

- one large-mouthed plastic bottle filled one-third of the way
- several smaller bottles, such as aspirin bottles
- three to four 7-inch cardboard squares
- eggs
- water balloons
- an apple

What You Do:

1. This is a variation of "Newton's Coin." Build you first tower as shown, with the large plastic bottle at the base (filled one-third of the way with water), the cardboard balanced on top of the large bottle, and the small aspirin bottle balanced on top of the cardboard.

2. Place the apple on top of the pill bottle. (See photo A.)

3. Now quickly strike the cardboard with a "finger flick" as you did in "Newton's Coin." (See photo B.)

Did the apple fall into the bottle? Did the cardboard fly off? Practice until you get it just right!

Now, for the real challenge:

1. Build a multilayer tower using the large bottle at the base and the cardboard sheets and pill bottles at **each** level as shown.

2. Now place an egg or a water balloon on the very top of your layered tower.

3. Get a friend, and each of you try to flick the four cardboards in the same direction at exactly the same time. Did the falling object make it into the large bottle at the bottom? The magic of science—and inertia!

Spinning Plate
The circus meets science!

Materials:
- The plate and balancing stick comes in this 'circus-themed' kit available through the Whirley-Whiley Company.

What You Do:

Using your wrist and not your arm, give the plate a firm yet steady spin, keeping it balanced on the stick. Continue to spin the plate as it begins to slow down. Break the world record: 108 plates spinning on sticks at the same time!

The Science:

Thank Newton again! In the natural world, moving objects typically remain in motion. Your plate is also balanced on its center of gravity, helping it stay in motion longer!

Fun Slides Carpet Skates
The twenty-first-century approach to sliding on your socks!

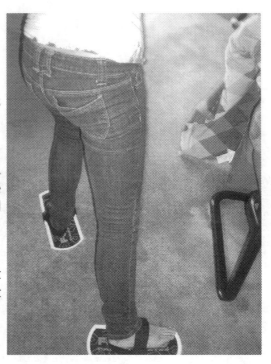

Materials:

- Pick up a pair of these super-fun carpet skates manufactured by Simtec.

What You Do:

Take a running start and just slide along the carpet. Make sure you move any dangerous or breakable objects so you have a clear path of several feet around where you are skating.

The Science:

The special plastic soles of the skates are resistant to friction and glide along any rug for several feet before stopping.

Go Extreme: Sock Slide

You may also experience this friction-reducing experience with a thin layer of socks made of polyester (plastic). Just slip on your polyester socks and try running and sliding. This works best on thin carpets.

Face-off Frenzy: Power-Band Hockey by Simtec

This fast-action game may become one of your favorites!

Materials:

- Buy this amazing portable air hockey game, which requires no extra anything!

What You Do:

Play this game anywhere—on carpets, on hardwood floors, or even outside on your driveway!

The Science:

Just like the Fun Slides Skates, this super-fun game relies on friction-resistant materials to get your puck moving.

Ghostly Rising

A group activity where excitement builds (and rises)!

What You Need:

• five to seven kids or teens

What You Do:

1. Have a volunteer stand perfectly straight and still.

2. Have each other person place two fingers at the various center-of-gravity locations of the standing volunteer as shown: One person in front of the "riser" with two fingers under the chin, two people with fingers at the back heels of the "riser's" feet, and two kids with fingertips under the "riser's" armpits.

3. When everyone is set in their positions, at the count of three, everyone lift using only their fingers. The "riser" should be lifted up at least a foot or two off the ground!

The Science:

Lifting in the above positions, the children are using the lifted child's center of gravity to their advantage, equally sharing the weight of the child. So while it seems you have called on some ghostly help, it is science that aids in what seems an impossible feat of weight lifting, using only people's fingertips!

Martian Bouncy Balls
How high can you bounce this out-of-this-world ball?

Materials:

- a new tennis ball
- thick, colorful rubber bands, available at an office supply store

What You Do:

1. Stretch the rubber bands and place them onto the tennis ball. After the first few, the process becomes much easier.

2. Count how many you can put on until you can no longer see the tennis ball. Try bouncing the sky-high ball after placing about one hundred bands on it.

3. See how many bands in total you can place on the ball. Now try bouncing your super ball!

4. Try launching your homemade sky-high ball from a basketball by simply dropping them both at the same time, with the smaller ball positioned on top of the larger ball..

The Science:

Your sky-high ball creation has more potential energy and kinetic (actual) energy stemming from the fact you have added layers of rubber bands.

Parallel World
Make yourself silly dizzy!

Materials:
- an extra large black (or colored black) card stock poster board
- a friend
- white markers or crayons
- a yardstick

What You Do:

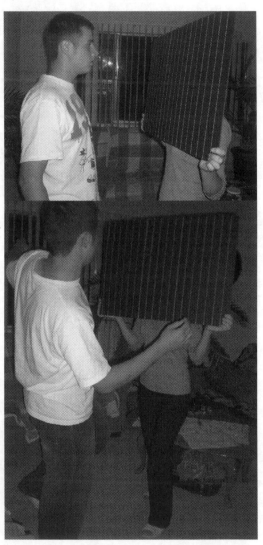

1. Using the yardstick as a guide, draw about fifteen to twenty straight, horizontal lines, each about two inches apart, on the poster board using your white colored marker or crayon. (You may also use white masking tape.)

2. Once your lines are drawn, have your friend hold the poster board horizontally.

3. Stand on one leg.

As your friend begins to move the board side to side, focus your stare at the lines on the board. What's happening?

The Science:

When we go about our daily lives, we subconsciously use stationary objects to keep us balanced. In this experiment, the moving board and parallel lines create the illusion that we ourselves are moving, and we become disoriented. This is why people get seasick from the motion of the ocean; on a boat, we lose our balance and any reference to stationary objects. You may have also experienced this phenomenon when a parked car near your parked car begins to move, and you mistakenly believe it is your car that is moving!

Paper Cup Mountain
You may want to capture this one on video!

Materials:

- 250 or more strong, 5-ounce paper cups
- seven to ten strong, 30-inch-square pieces of cardboard cut from boxes
- a crowd!
- thick grass or safe ground covering

What You Do:

1. Arrange the cups lid-down in a square formation consisting of twenty-five cups (five rows of five cups each).

2. Align a cardboard sheet on top of your formation of twenty-five cups.

3. Have someone stand on top of the cups carefully without disturbing the arrangement.

4. Continue to build with 25 cups on each additional layer. Try standing on each level, ensuring that the tower remains centered and all cups stay in place to prevent a faulty tower.

5. Assist your mountain seeker in getting on and off the tower as the building progresses. You may want to have a person hold each side of the tower to prevent gravity from winning! How high can you go?

The Science:

The cylinder-shaped cups are very strong. In fact, each cup can hold about fifteen pounds of weight. (Try placing a small, heavy object on one cup!) Once your tower becomes many levels high, gravity and imprecise construction can cause it to come crashing down!

Paper Tower

Turn flimsy paper into strong towers!

Materials:
- two sheets of newspaper
- scissors
- optional: Scotch tape

What to do:

Using only the two sheets of newspaper, cut out shapes and build the tallest tower possible. Try building using your creativity, paper, scissors and no further instruction!

The Science;

The lightweight newspaper must be folded into strong supporting shapes, such as triangles and squares, to help support the tower against the forces of gravity!

CHAPTER 4: SKY HIGH

Sky Party Balloons
Into the wild blue yonder!

Materials:
- a small helium tank
- five to ten super-sized quality helium balloons
- string
- permanent markers

What You Do:

1. Fill each of your super-sized balloons with helium. Tie a string around each one after filling.

2. Draw faces, pictures, names, etc., on your balloons using various colorful permanent markers!

3. Let the balloons go, one at a time or all at once!

4. Now that's a sky party! Great photo op!

The Science:

Helium gas is lighter than the surrounding gasses in the atmosphere, therefore it rises up, up, and away! Try tying a ball of tissue paper to the balloon to see how the extra weight affects your balloon's flight!

Flying Fish
Big fun with a little scrap of paper!

Materials:
- a strip of paper 2.5 inches by 7 inches
- markers or crayons
- scissors

What You Do:

1. Cut slits on opposite sides of your strip of paper about a half inch from each end.

2. Decorate your "fish" with markers or crayons.

3. Connect the two slits together to form what looks like a fish tail.

4. Toss around your new creation in the house, or find a nice place with a good wind where you can toss it high and watch the breeze help it along!

The Science:

Your new creation spins wildly as aerodynamics act upon the unusually shaped, spherical fish!

Go Extreme: Big Fish!

Try making a giant fish by experimenting with different sizes of scrap paper. Use ratios to the above numbers. For example, double the size to create a five-inch by fourteen-inch super-sized fish!

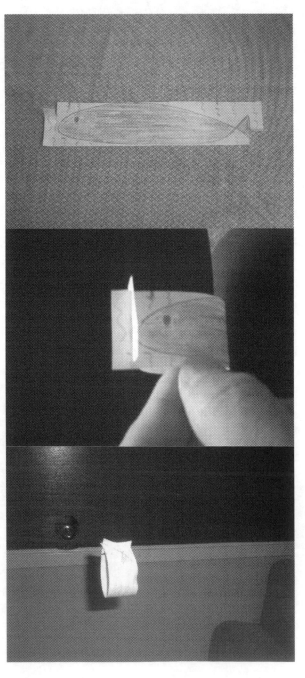

Walk-Along Glider

With practice and patience, you can create this truly "magical" glider!

Materials and Preparation:
- a page from phone book
- scissors
- sturdy cardboard poster board, a minimum of 25 inches square

What You Do:

1. Cut out a page from a phone book. Cut it so it's four and a half inches long and one inch wide.

2. Make a crisp ninety-degree fold upward. Without disturbing these angled edges, fold one length wide section crisply upward at a forty-five-degree angle to your glider.

3. On the opposite lengthwise side, fold crisply downward at a forty-five-degree angle.

4. Hold the glider as high above your head as possible and simply let go. The glider should start spinning as you walk underneath it and slightly behind, following its linear path!

The Science:

You are providing the right amount of "lift" as you walk along behind your magnificent gravity-defying glider!

UFO Solar Balloon!

Hold on to this amazing, solar-energized UFO!

Materials:
- one large, lightweight black bag
- string
- several people

What to do:

Get yourself a black "solar" bag known as the "UFO Solar Balloon," manufactured by ToySmith. The cost is around ten dollars. Simply tie a knot in one end and run around gathering gasses (air) with the open end of the bag. Once you have it filled at least 90 percent, tie off the second end of the bag. Tie a sturdy string to one end. Now you can either have several people give it a nice toss up as illustrated or simply rest it on the ground and witness firsthand the power of solar energy!

The Science:

The recipe for a great flight: the lightweight, energy-loving black bag, a hot day, and solar energy. This combination allows your UFO to float into the heavens … except the string you are holding should keep it in the stratosphere!

UFO Liftoff
This "real" flying UFO spins and dazzles!

Materials:

- One remote controlled UFO (recommended: one made by SpinMaster or a light-up version found at Handhelditems.com. The cost is around twenty-five dollars.)

What You Do:

This pie-sized UFO flies great indoors and even better outside. In addition to the instructions, I highly recommend to start slowly, easing on and off the trigger until you get the hang of it. Outside, the UFO will honestly fly up to seventy-five yards. Make sure to point the infrared light transmitter toward the UFO at all times, as this controls the flight.

Activity Zone!

*Launch your UFO to record-breaking heights!

*Control the movement of the r/c UFO by pointing the infrared light controller in various directions.

The Science:

The infrared transmitter sends a signal to control the flight of the UFO. The UFO "spins" just like a helicopter. Its small, powerful engine is aided by rotating blades that push against a cushion of gasses (air) to achieve upward motion—every action creates an equal and opposite reaction!

UFO Balloon

UFO excitement for less than a dollar!

Materials:

- The seventy-nine-cent "UFO Saucer Balloon" (Is it possible to have this much fun for seventy-nine cents? Yes, yes, and *yes*! The Flying Saucer Balloon is more fun than almost any other flying toy that costs one hundred times more than this little gem.)

What You Do:

Simply blow up the flying saucer and toss it in the air. It will spin and move like crazy as air escapes out the side. Use it over and over again.

You can find the UFO Saucer at magic stores, some party stores, and online if you search for "The Flying Saucer Balloon."

Activity Zone:

*Count how many revolutions your balloon UFO makes.

*Note whose UFO spins the longest.

*Toss it high and predict where it will land!

The Science:

Air is the fuel that spins the balloon like a UFO.

Hoops and Loops Wind-Cutter
A versatile flyer that really works!

Materials:
- One 3-by-5-inch card
- markers
- Scotch tape
- scissors
- a straw

What You Do:

1. Cut three even strips lengthwise from your three-by-five-inch card.

2. Decorate your mini-flyer as in photo A.

3. Tape the first strip into a hoop on both sides as shown in photo B.

4. Next, tape your two remaining strips together to form one larger hoop as shown in photo C. Make sure to tape on both sides for aerodynamic purposes!

5. Tape the smaller hoop to the front of the straw as shown in photo D.

6. Securely tape the larger hoop near the back of the straw lined up with the front hoop as shown in photo E.

7. Toss the wind-cutter straight like a dart; try tossing from both ends.

Go Extreme: "Elite Loopster"

1. Add another straw and add a giant hoop to your wind-cutter and observe your results!

2. Add tissue paper, and even more straws and hoops!

3. Toss your wind-cutter at an angle. Measure for distance! Go for looping action!

The Science:

The laws of aerodynamics (gravity, drag resistance, lift, and thrust) all act upon your flight creation. The shape of the hoops helps your wind-cutter resist the force of drag.

Ricochet Launcher
An "outer-space-seeking" experiment!

Materials:
- a well-pumped basketball
- a new tennis ball

What You Do:

1. Place the tennis ball on top of the basketball.

2. Allow the tennis ball and basketball to fall together "as one" onto a hard surface. Wow! Where did it go?

The Science;

The mass of the basketball accelerates the tennis ball. The same principle, known as conservation of momentum, helps a tennis player smash a tennis ball 100 miles per hour using a stringed racket.

Try using a super-ball with your basketball launcher!

Astro Launcher

Shoot for the moon!

Materials and Preparation:
- a super large and well-inflated rubber bouncy ball at least 40 inches in diameter

What You Do:

Standing on a chair, rest your basketball and tennis ball on top of your super large rubber ball. Holding all three balls together with a friend, count down three, two, one … and let go!

Now how high and far did your balls travel?

The Science:

By adding a third ball, the transfer of energy is increased, and the launches more amazing!

Go Extreme: Astro-Egg

Try launching a raw egg from your launcher and catching it before …

Backyard Flyer

A durable flyer for hours of enjoyment!

Materials:
- a BackYard Flyer toy, made by KidGalaxy

What You Do:

Follow the instructions. Make sure to handle the durable airplane gently!

Activities Zone!

*How many circles can you make with your Backyard Flyer?

*Try landing your Backyard Flyer in a pre-determined landing area!

The Science:

The plane gets lift from the surrounding air and thrust from its small battery-powered engine. The wings help with lift as well!

World Record Aerobie Disc
Stand back—way back!

Materials:
- one Aerobie World Record Disc toy

What You Do:

With a flick of the wrist along a very straight path, toss your disc. Go for your own personal disc-throwing record!

Activity Zone

*Compare your other flying objects with the flight of your Aerobie!

*Go for distance, targets, speed and so much more!

The Science:

The Aerobie Disc is created with very thin, yet strong plastic with elevated "lips" that allow it to maintain lift in center of the disc, thus allowing for maximum speed and minimum drag.

SlingWings

A combination of a catapult and an airplane, this toy makes for a fun afternoon of flight!

Materials:

• a set of SlingWings, manufactured by the SlingWings Company

What You Do:

Launch your SlingWings into the air using the catapult device that is included.

Activity Zone!

*Try filling the skies with as many SlingWings as you can simultaneously!

*Count how many seconds your SlingWings remain in the air.

*Air wars! Battle others with multiple launches! Last one in flight is the winner!

The Science:

The power of thrust allows your SlingWings to reach a good height before the wings open for a free flight buoyed by air pressure and lift.

UFO Toss-up
A new ball game with star power!

Materials:

- a 40-inch-diameter or larger latex or helium balloon
- friends

What You Do:

Fill your super large balloon half full of regular air, and fill it the rest of the way with helium (available at a full-service grocery store where they sell flowers and balloons). Go to a wide open park and start tossing your balloon around. Great for the games "keep away," "three flies up," or your own inventive game!

Activity Zone!

* Great for the games "keep away," "three flies up," or your own inventive game!

The Science:

The helium, being lighter than the surrounding atmospheric gasses, will get the balloon up in the air. The other gasses that fill your balloon are a mixture of oxygen, nitrogen, carbon dioxide, and other heavier gasses that will eventually bring the giant balloon down to earth

Go Extreme: Space UFO-Make Alien Contact!

Add a little more helium and your balloon may sail off over your nearest hill or buildings into the wild blue yonder! Take pictures of your UFO as it floats above the horizon!

UFO in Your Room

Experiment to get this UFO to fly right!

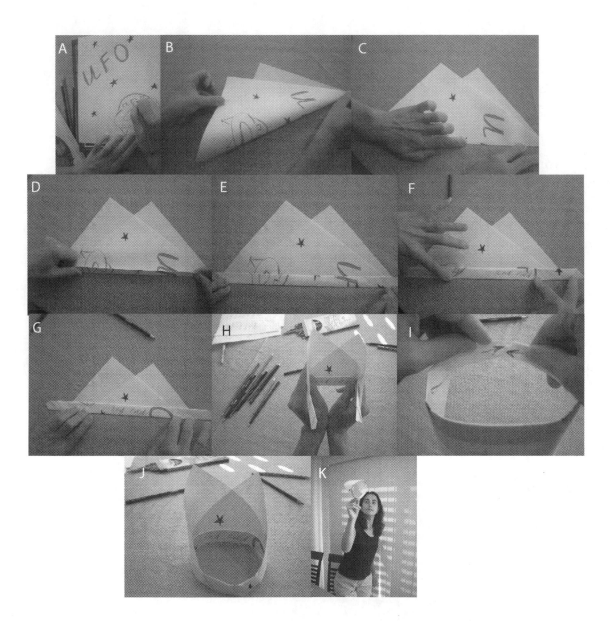

Materials:
- markers
- a sheet of copy paper, 8 1/2 by 11 inches

What You Do:

1. Decorate both sides of your paper as you wish as shown in photo A.

2. Fold the paper following the photo sequence: Your first fold creates twin peaks as shown in photos B and C. Your next three folds should be three one-inch folds up from the bottom, all with precise creases as shown in photos D, E, F, and G.

3. Shaping your UFO into a half circle, simply put together the ends into the slots as shown in photos H and I. Tape the ends together if you wish. Now, hold the UFO with the "wind-dicing" cylinder in front and toss it gently in a straight path as shown.

The Science:

You have created a lightweight cylindrical flyer that cuts through the air effortlessly. In fact, you have quite an aerodynamically agile UFO that defies gravity and drag resistance—at least for a trip across the family room!

Go Extreme: "Super-Sized Helicopter"

Try building your giant helicopter to achieve lift!

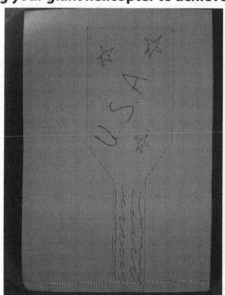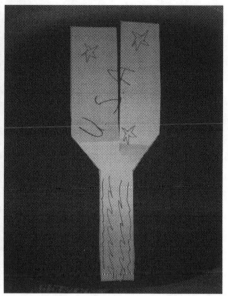

Materials:
- a large sheet of white copy paper, at least 8 ½ by 17 inches
- scissors
- paperclips
- crayons or markers

What You Do:
1. Looking at the photo to help you, draw and cut out a helicopter seven inches long, three inches at the angle, and seven more inches from top of the angle to the top of copter. Your copter should also be two inches wide at the very bottom and four and a half inches wide at the top.
2. Decorate your copter with markers and pens.
3. Cut out the drawing, making sure to cut down the middle, creating two rotors.
4. Fold back the rotors, one forward and one backward.
5. Secure two or more paperclips to the bottom middle of your copter, and toss your gigantic flyer outside in windy conditions!

The Science:

Your paper flyer is affected by the movement of air pushing against both rotors. Gravity also plays a role, as does lift from the wind!

CHAPTER 5: ROCKET POWER

Paper Rocket
A great pocket rocket!

Materials and Preparation:
- an unsharpened pencil
- a strip of paper 2 inches wide and 7 inches long
- markers
- tape
- scissors
- a nonflexible straw

What You Do:

1. Decorate your paper to be flight ready as in photo A.

2. Position your paper so that its long side is horizontal. Then wrap it tightly around the pencil at about a thirty-degree angle as shown in photo B.

3. Tape the rocket in two or three places so the paper will be held in place.

4. Fold down the top as shown in photo C.

5. If you desire, make fins and tape them onto the base of your paper rocket.

6. Push the straw into the rocket.

7 Blow into your straw to send your new rocket sky high! (See photo D.)

The Science:

You have just assembled a simple rocket with an invisible layer of gasses as your fuel. Newton's Law stating that "every action has a reaction" is also at play. Thrust your rocket by blowing through your straw.

Alka-Seltzer Rocket
A rocket you can launch on the go!

Materials and Preparation:

- one Fuji Film canister, empty and clean
- a few pieces of broken Alka-Seltzer tablets
- 1/8 cup of water
- permanent markers
- optional: baking soda and vinegar

What You Do:

1. Decorate your little rocket using permanent markers.

2. Fill the film canister a quarter of the way full of water.

3. Drop one to two small pieces of Alka-Seltzer tablets into the canister and close the lid quickly.

4. Place the canister with the lid side flat on the ground, the palm of your hand, or even your head! Wait for it! Blastoff!

Activity Zone!

*Also try placing two prepped bottles lid-to-lid on the ground

*Place one on top of the other!

*Try using more or less water.

*Try putting two **full** tablets inside!

*Try adding one ounce of vinegar and half a teaspoon of baking soda, and close lid quickly!)

The Science:

The Alka-Seltzer and water mixture creates a gas inside the canister that cannot stay trapped forever! As the gas expands, the lid is pressured open, and the eruption that follows sends your little rocket skyward!

Soda Rocket

Perhaps the world's most famous experiment.

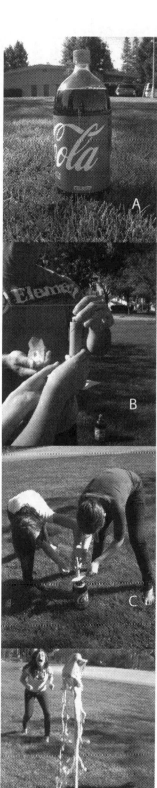

Materials and preparation:

1. Pick up a two-liter bottle of Diet Coke or Pepsi and one bottle of regular Coke or Pepsi.

2. Roll a 3-by-5-inch index card into a tube large enough to hold seven Mentos candies. Tape the tube together in three places to ensure it is nice and stable. (See photo A.)

What You Do:

1. Drop the candies into your tube and hold them in place using a flat three-by-five-inch index card as shown in photo B.

2. Open up the lid on your soda bottle without spilling any of the carbonated liquid.

3. Line up the opening of your tube with the opening of the bottle and quickly remove the flat three-by-five-inch card, allowing the candies to fall into the opening of your soda bottle. (See photo C.)

4. Standing close to the bottle may produce a soda shower! (See photo D.)

Activity Zone!

*Line up several sodas and launch all at once with friends and family.

*Take photos and/or videos.

*Open a soda bottle and wait a few minutes before dropping in the Mentos mints! Observe the reaction!

*Drop in other mints or candies to see if the reaction is the same or different.

The Science:

As of this writing, scientists are not exactly sure why the soda shoots out like a liquid rocket; it is hypothesized that the reaction has something to do with the little holes in the candy and the carbon dioxide gas that give sodas their fizz!

Moon Shoes

Young scientists can't get enough of these mini bouncers!

Materials:
- Moon Shoes by Hart Toys
- your own tennis shoes or athletic shoes

What You Do:

Get out on the grass and start bouncing!

Activity Zone!

*Have a long jump contest!

*Have a high jump contest!

*Have a relay race with multiple Moon Shoes!

The Science:

The Moon Shoes toy works on the idea of potential energy stored inside the shoes' elastic bands, which exhibit actual kinetic energy after being stretched before releasing their energy.

Olympics on Mercury

Out-of-this-world fun!

Materials:

- handheld air-powered rockets at a toy or hobby store
- three 50-foot tape measures
- a scale
- Rocket formula: H = 15(t/2)2; H = Height, T = Time in seconds.
- Count how many seconds from launch to landing. For example, if from launch to landing took 8 seconds: 8 ÷ 2 = 4 × 2 = 8 × 15 = 120 feet!
- Stomp Rocket or other launch rocket – young people – yardstick, stuck firmly a few inches into the ground

What You Do:

Lay out all three of your cloth or metal fifty- or one-hundred-foot tape measures, all stretched out to fifty feet or more and about twenty yards apart Stick your yardstick firmly into the ground about fifteen yards from any obstacles.

Mercury Station #1: Long Jump. How far can you jump on Mercury? Calculate earth's distance and multiply by 2.7 to get an accurate reading on Mercury!

Mercury Station #2: High Jump. How high can you jump on Mercury? As above, calculate your height on earth by multiplying by 2.7 to get a reading as if you were jumping on Mercury!

Mercury Station #3: Stomp Rocket Launch. Launch your rocket for height by using your rocket calculation from above to figure out your launch on earth. Then multiply by 2.7 to get your height on Mercury!

Mercury Station #4: Weight on Mercury. Multiply your weight on earth using the scale and then multiply it by 0.37 to get your weight on Mercury! Now that's a fast diet!

Mercury Station #5: Air Pump Rocket Shot. Using one of your tape measures, launch your rocket for distance, record your earthly numbers, and then multiply by—you guessed it—2.7 to obtain the distance your rocket would have gone on Mercury!

The Science:

If you were able to withstand Mercury's very hot temperatures, you would experience two-thirds less gravity there than on earth! I guess this would make you the new Olympic champion—at least on planet Mercury!

Happy Birthday on Venus

Make yourself younger or older anytime, thanks to the stars and the planets!

Look at the chart to calculate your age on any planet in our solar system.

Materials:

- the chart shown above
- a calculator
- a pencil
- paper

What You Do:

1. Put your age into the calculator.

2. Press the divide symbol and then put in your chosen planet's period of revolution around the sun.

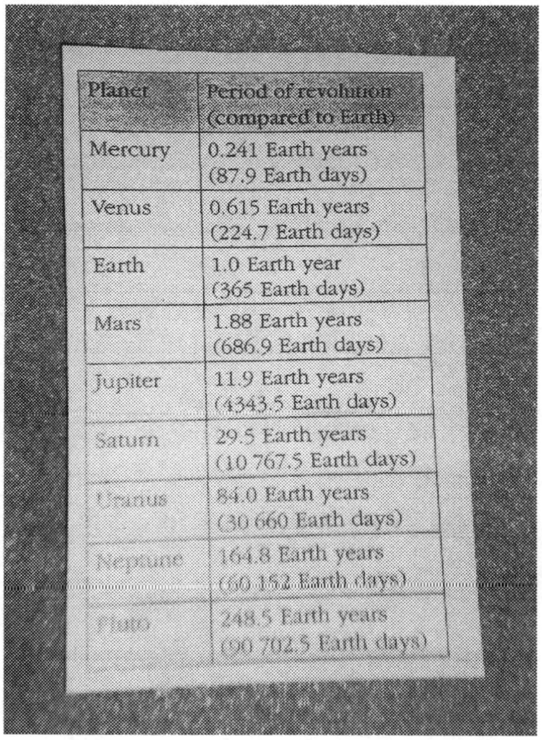

For example, let's say you chose Jupiter and you're fourteen years old. You would calculate 14 ÷ 11.9 (Jupiter's earth years.) Your age on Jupiter? Just over a year old!

The Science:

We earthlings calculate one year as being 365 days, which is the time it takes for the earth to revolve completely around the sun. Of course, the earth rotates every twenty-four hours—an earth day! All planets orbit the sun differently due to size, distance from the sun and other factors.

Planet	Period of revolution (compared to Earth)
Mercury	0.241 Earth years (87.9 Earth days)
Venus	0.615 Earth years (224.7 Earth days)
Earth	1.0 Earth year (365 Earth days)
Mars	1.88 Earth years (686.9 Earth days)
Jupiter	11.9 Earth years (4343.5 Earth days)
Saturn	29.5 Earth years (10 767.5 Earth days)
Uranus	84.0 Earth years (30 660 Earth days)
Neptune	164.8 Earth years (60 152 Earth days)
Pluto	248.5 Earth years (90 702.5 Earth days)

Rocket Balloons
Try catching these amazing rockets!

Materials:
- "Rocket Balloons," available at almost any party or toy store

What You Do:
1. Get the hang of launching these amazing, whistling, flying balloons.
2. Try catching them as they zigzag, dip, and soar just out of the reach of your outstretched hands!

Activity Zone!

*Catch the balloons before they hit the ground.

*Take a picture of your balloon rockets.

The Science:

A Rocket Balloon is powered by the air that escapes from its opening. Every action has an opposite and equal reaction as the rocket balloons launch into an atmosphere.

Stomp Rockets

How high did yours go?

Welcome to the amazing world of Stomp Rockets!

Materials:

- Stomp Rockets, made by D and L Company
- a large grassy area

What You Do:

Try launching these amazing air-powered rockets for height and distance.

Calculate the height your rocket would have gone on Mercury by the rocket formula found in the "Olympics on Mercury" experiment.

The Science:

Conservation of momentum, or the principle of an object (in this case, gasses) accelerating the motion of another object (the rocket), is at play in this experiment. Gravity and drag finally slow down this skyscraper!

Air Burst Rockets'
Perhaps the highest-flying air rocket in the world!

Materials:
- a set of Air Burst Rockets
- a large, safe, grassy area

What You Do:

Blast off this sky-high rocket extra safely by following the instructions, step by step. **Never** put your face near the rocket while it is on the rocket base!

The Science:

Just as in the Stomp Rocket experiment above, Air Burst Rockets work as air—the atmosphere's sea of gasses—quickly travels upward toward the light, aerodynamic rocket, sending it rapidly sky-high!

Titan Water Rocket by Banzai
Put on a spectacular water rocket show!

Materials:

- a Titan Water Rocket

What You Do:

You must follow every step exactly in order for this most amazing rocket to launch effectively! Still, even if the rocket does not launch on every attempt, the excitement in anticipation proves that the journey is the reward!

Activity Zone!

*Count how many seconds your rocket stays in the air!

*Try to catch your Titan!

*Stand near the launch site and get soaked!

*Take a picture or video of your Titan!

The Science:

As in many of our rocket experiments, fast-moving air provides the fuel. The spraying water simply adds to the exciting action!

CHAPTER 6: SCIENCE STUNTS, PUZZLES, AND CHALLENGES

Fickle Finger
A perplexing view of the world!

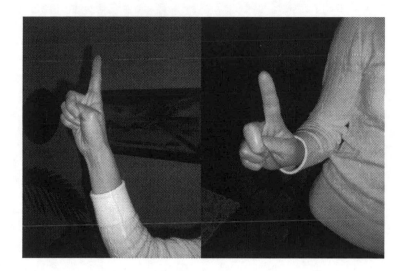

Materials:
- your pointer finger
- a friend

What You Do:

1. With only the pointer finger of your right hand pointed upward, begin a level, clockwise rotation as you slowly move your right hand down below your line of vision while still maintaining the clockwise motion. Your friend should focus only on the clockwise motion of your finger.

2. As your finger continues its motion and as your hand slowly drops below eye level, your clock will mysteriously be moving counterclockwise!!!

Challenge your friend to perform the same science stunt for your eyes!

The Science:

This experiment is an example of perception science. From below, your finger moves clockwise, from above, counterclockwise. A good example is when you look out from an airplane window, the moving cars look like kid's toys, yet we know they are much larger close up. This is a type of perception science.

Toe Writing

How fast can you write your name?

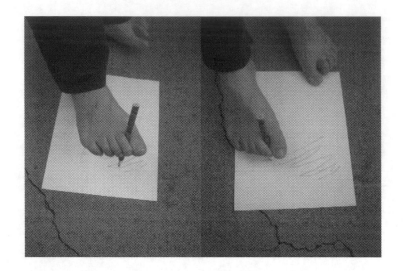

Materials:
- your toes
- assorted sizes and colors of markers and/or crayons
- a large tablet of paper

What You Do:

1. First, try writing something using your hand. Easy, right?

2. Now, close your eyes and write with your hand.

3. Now for a challenge, open your eyes, place a marker between your toes, and try writing a sentence or drawing a picture.

The biggest challenge: Try writing or drawing with your toes while your eyes are closed.

Compare all four methods of drawing!

The Science:

Of course, writing with our hands is easy and natural because we are well practiced in it. Even when you wrote with your hands while your eyes were closed, you probably did an adequate job. Yet, using our toes certainly throws a curveball into our writing and drawing efforts. We are naturally not set up to use our toes to draw, and it's worse yet when we attempt to do so with our eyes closed! It is kind of like walking on our hands; we just don't get very far!

Anti-gravity Kids
Float three feet off the ground!

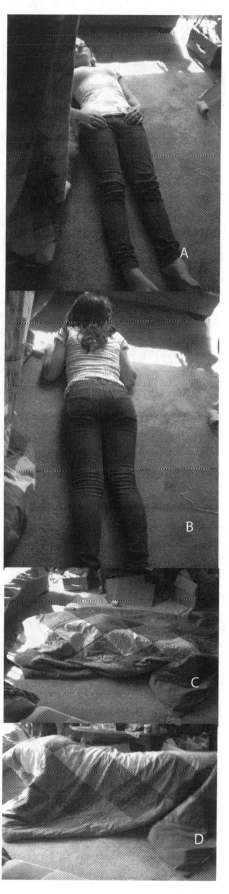

Materials:

- an assistant
- a large blanket to cover the assistant
- a clear area, such as grass or a carpeted room

What You Do:

Have your assistant practice:

1. Lying on their back as you hold the blanket out in front, blocking their body from your audience so it is fully covered by the blanket as shown in photo A.

2. As soon as the blanket goes in front of their body, your assistant should secretly roll over onto their stomach as shown in photo B.

3. Cover your assistant completely while they secretly bend their arms to do a push-up. Keeping their head facedown, they very slowly extend their arms into a push-up. At the same time, they rise up onto their left shin so that their left knee to their left foot is resting on the ground.

4. Next, they lift their right leg straight and extend it back. Their body should "rise" as a straight line, from his head all the way to the end of their right foot, level and parallel to the ground as shown in photos C and D. From the audience's viewpoint, your assistant has just floated two to four feet off the ground!

*Practice this experiment at least twenty times!

The Science:

This is a classic optical illusion. The brain knows people can never conquer the force of gravity, yet the eyes view such a feat!

Bottle and Straw Challenge
Challenge your friends!

Materials:
- a 12- to 16-ounce glass soda bottle
- a nonflexible straw

What You Do:

1. Challenge anyone to pick up the bottle using only the straw—nothing else can touch the bottle!

Show the solution: Bend the straw one-third of the way from the bottom and push the bent straw into bottle. As it springs upward, the straw will lock into place, allowing you to lift the bottle!

Piranha Puzzle Challenge
Something fishy is going on here!

Materials:
- eight popsicle sticks (You may also use super-large colorful craft sticks as an alternative.)

What You Do:

1. Create a fish picture with the sticks as shown in photo A.
2. Challenge a friend to have the fish swimming in the opposite direction by moving only three sticks.
3. Show the solution: see the three moves in the sequenced illustrations in photos B, C, and D.

The Science:

The brain cannot initially process the reverse image of the fish; this is too much information and confuses the brain. Only after a logical and step-by-step process is the brain able to figure out this fishy puzzler!

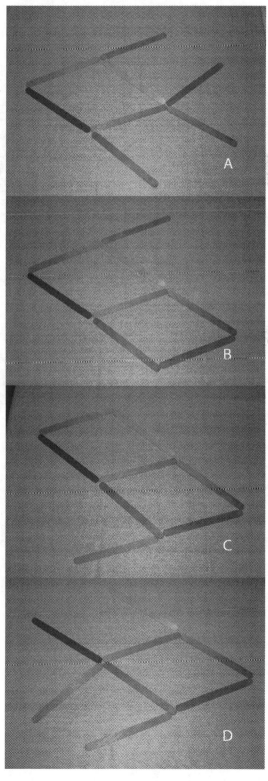

Air Power
You vs. air!

Materials:
- two plungers
- two people

What You Do:

1. Align the open ends of two plungers perfectly and push them together.

2. Standing face to face, one person grasps the wooden pole of one plunger while you hold the wooden pole of your plunger.

3. Try to pull the two plungers apart by pushing the poles toward one another.

The Science:

The two plungers remain vacuum sealed together. The air pressure inside the plungers is stronger than the two people who are pulling on the plungers.

How to separate the plungers:

Simply slide one plunger over the other as shown in the illustration!

Walk Through Paper

Win this bet every time!

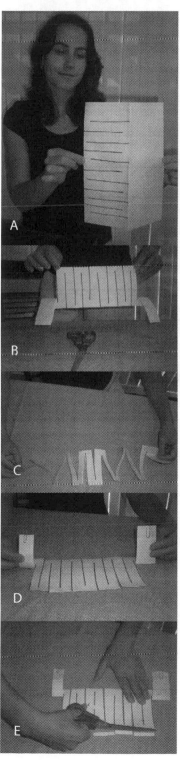

Materials:

- safety scissors
- crayons or markers
- one sheet of plain white copy paper; decorate it on both sides, if desired

What You Do:

1. Fold the paper in half as shown in photo A.

2. From the folded edge, make two cuts toward the opposite edges as shown in photo B. Be careful not to cut through the opposite edges of the paper.

3. Working only from the inside of the cuts you have just made, cut slits about one inch apart, first from the bottom edge and then from the top edge as shown in photo C. Be very careful not to cut through to the opposite edges of the paper—leave about half an inch from the edges!

4. Finally, cut along the folded edges between your first two cuts as shown in photos D, E, and F. Carefully open up your intact, giant hole and walk through!

The Science:

You have created a hole one can walk through by cutting on the insides of all the edges of your paper!

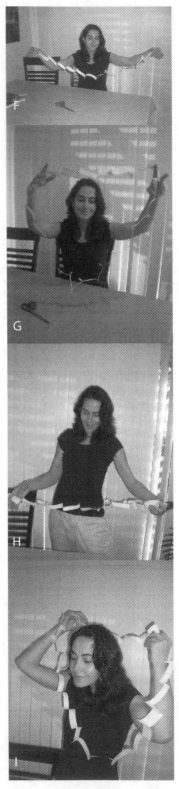

Walking On Your Head
Seeing is believing!

Materials:

- a handheld mirror

What You Do:

1. Simply hold your mirror about seven inches over your head, yet so you can still see it. The mirror should be flat and so the image faces the ground.

2. Start walking and take a glance at the mirror. The illusion will make it appear you are walking on your head!

The Science:

The image is an illusion that confuses the brain into believing the message your eyes are receiving: the impossibility of walking on your head!

Cotton Candy Pasta Tower
Create your own leaning tower!

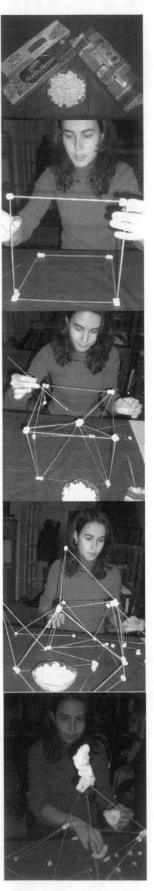

Materials:
- various uncooked long pastas, including fettuccini, spaghetti, and angel hair, for example
- small and large marshmallows
- cotton candy

What You Do:

1. Use large marshmallows as your base as you stick the various pastas into them.

2. Build your tower with shapes, continuing to connect the larger, heavier pastas at the bottom of your tower and lighter pastas and smaller marshmallows near the top! Add cotton candy to cover your architectural wonder!

The Science:

Planning, designed shapes and sizes, construction materials and methods, and the effects of gravity and inertia are all contributing factors in the final appearance and stability of your architectural masterpiece!

Amazing Arch
Solve this puzzling architectural wonder!

Materials:
- About twenty square cardboard boxes, all the same size
- friends
- optional: a photo of a Roman arch to use as a guide

What You Do:

1. With many helping hands, attempt to build a free-standing, kid-sized arch out of boxes!

2. Try putting each progressive box a few inches over the edge of the box below it, creating the arch shape.

The Science:

Similar to rock balancing, building the amazing arch relies on finding its center of gravity and placing the boxes so they are supportive and balanced together!

Rising Golf Ball
Are you up for the challenge?

Materials:
- a golf ball
- a jar with a cap
- some rice

What You Do:

1. Place the golf ball at the bottom of the jar and cover it with rice.

2. Close the jar and attempt to get the ball to the top of the rice without opening the jar and without turning the jar sideways or upside down!

The Secret and the Science:

The law of displacement states that larger objects displace, or move, smaller objects. By shaking the bottle up and down, the rice is displaced as the golf ball eventually rises to the top of the moved rice!

Seven-Straw Sipping Challenge
A challenge never tasted so good!

Materials:

- seven straws
- a beverage of your choice
- a glass

What You Do:

1. Fill your glass nearly to the top with a beverage.

2. Place one straw in your glass and see how fast you can drink the entire beverage. Pretty quickly, right?

3. Now place one straw into your beverage and hold the other 6 in your hand, in a bundle, outside the glass (at the same height as the straw that's in the liquid).

4. Place all seven straws in your mouth and begin sucking on all of them. How hard is it to drink now?

The Science:

Drinking with only one straw is easy, because air pressure is limited . But when you add six more straws, the air pressure surrounding you is working against you, as you swallow much more air than liquid! With all that swallowed gas, a burping contest may ensue!

Hyper-Shake Soda

Shake things up with erupting soda!

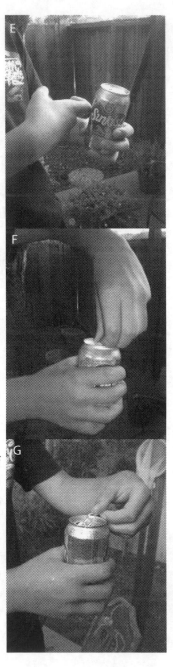

Materials:

• two unopened cans of soda, placed out in the sun for an hour ahead of the experiment, if possible

What You Do:

1. Shake your first can of soda as madly as possible for about a minute. (See photo B)

2. Point the can away from your face as you open it quickly! A soda can volcano! (See photo C)

3. Now do the same with the second can, shaking it up and down wildly, but do not open it yet! (See photo D)

4. Tap the side of the can seven times quickly and then open it! What, no volcano? (See photos E, F and G)

The Science:

The first soda erupted in a stream of excited carbon dioxide gas that was contained in the can. The second soda's carbon dioxide bubbles were calmed down by the tapping of your fingers, resulting in the anticlimactic opening of the can. At least you can drink the second one!

Extreme Reflex

Catch it if you can!

Materials and Preparation:

- a sheet of thick poster board, available at a craft store
- markers
- scissors
- a friend

1. Draw a set of horizontal lines on your poster board, evenly spaced every 5 inches.

2. Write a word, such as "awesome," "great," "good," or "terrific" near the bottom of the board, just over the lines you have drawn.

3. In the middle of the board, write words like "okay," "so-so," "not bad," etc. Near the top, write words like "try again," "are you joking?" "sad," and so on. You may want to add pictures relating to the words, such as an unhappy face toward the top of your homemade reflex meter.

What You Do:

1. Now get a friend to try your reflex meter.

2. Your volunteer should open up their hand right as you set the bottom of your meter just above the curved hand in catching position.

3. Let the meter drop at random times and have your friend try to catch it as quickly as he or she can!

The Science:

It takes a person less than a split second to react to the falling meter. First, the eyes must send the message to the brain, which sends the message to the body, which then must react by catching the meter.

Go Extreme: Blind Reflexes!

Have your volunteer close his or her eyes and call out when you are dropping the meter. See if their reaction time is quicker or slower.

Bernoulli's Bag Blow-up
Blow up the bag with just one breath!

Materials:
- a set of Bernoulli's Bags, available from www.SteveSpanglerScience.com

What You Do:

1. Try blowing up the bag with one breath of air.

The Secret:

1. Open up the bag.

2. Hold the mouth of the bag wide open and about ten inches from your mouth.

3. Take a deep breath all the way into your lungs and then exhale, strong and steady, into the balloon. This one long breath can blow up the bag fully.

The Science:

Using Bernoulli's Principle, air pressure creates a vacuum of air that is sucked into the bag. So in reality, it is the movement of air all around you that fills the balloon! Bernoulli's Principle also describes how airplanes stay aloft, as the movement of air over the wings is faster than the movement of air under the wings of planes. The principle is also helpful in putting out fires by removing oxygen and in filling blimps quickly.

Confuse Yourself
A self puzzler!

Materials:
- your two hands
- a friend

What You Do:

1. Hold your hands straight out in front of you so they are touching back to back.

2. Cross your right arm over your left arm and clasp your hands as shown in photos A and B.

3. Keeping your hands clasped, swing your arms and hands all around until your hands end up directly in front of your chin as shown in photo C. Do this, as shown, in one circular motion.

4. Ask a friend to point toward one of your fingers without touching it.

5. Try to move that finger—and only that finger—on the first try. (See photo D.) Nearly impossible, huh?

6. Try it again, but now ask your friend to touch any one finger. Is it easier now?

The Science:

With your fingers and hands in a kind of tangled puzzle, your brain is confused, even though you can see the finger you want to move. When your finger is touched, your brain solves the tactile illusion puzzle and aids with you moving the correct finger.

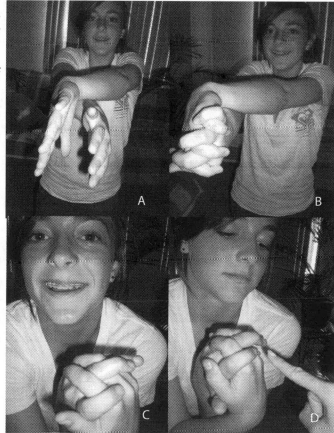

CHAPTER 7: SCIENCE MAGIC AND ILLUSION

Colors and Words Madness
Your brain may never be the same!

Materials:
- several different colored crayons or markers
- a sheet of plain white paper
- a friend or two

What You Do:

1. Ask each volunteer to write down at least fifteen color words, such as blue, green, magenta, gold, etc. The color words must be written in a different color than the word's color. For example, your friend may write the word *blue* with a red crayon, the word *green* with a yellow crayon, and so on. They may use any color as long as it does not match the color word that is written.

2. Trade papers and have your friends read off the words they see. Keep track of how long it takes them to do so. Easy and fast, right?

3. Now ask your friends to read off the actual colors they see. Much more difficult, right?

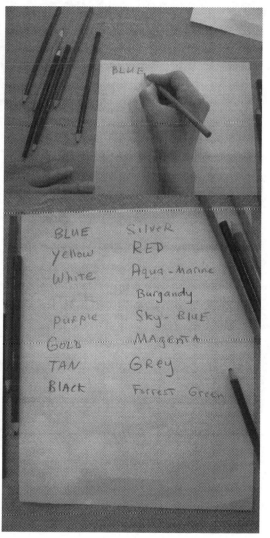

The Science:

We are well practiced in reading words, and this is not difficult. Yet when we see both the color and the written word, the brain attempts to read the word but is told to also recognize the color, so the brain is confused for a moment as it processes both the word and the color simultaneously. Try having two friends speak to you at the same time, nonstop, for one minute, and record how much of each one's dialogue you can process and remember.

Light-headed!
Now that's using your head!

Materials:

- a 15-watt twisty florescent light bulb
- one 12 inch or larger helium balloon
- a darkened room
- a good head of hair

What You Do:

1. Hold the light bulb in one hand and vigorously rub your head about twenty times back and forth on a balloon that is tied to your other hand.

2. Touch the area of the balloon you rubbed on your head to the metal part of the light bulb.

You should see a ghostly glow!

The Science:

The static energy you created became current electricity as it flowed from the balloon to the light bulb, which excited the gas inside and lit up the bulb! Continuing to rub the energized balloon to metal conductors (which allow energy to flow) creates a mini light show!

Balloon Pinata

Science magic, or magical science? You decide!

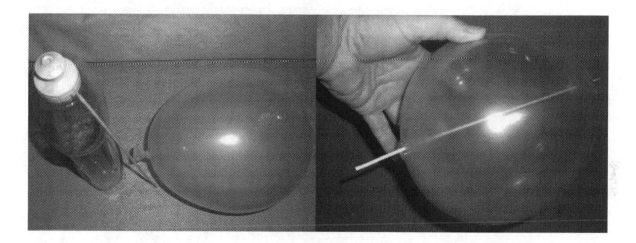

Materials and Preparation:
- a wooden skewer
- Cooking oil
- thick latex balloons
- confetti or very small, wrapped candies
- Apply a thin coat of the cooking oil evenly all over the skewer..

Fill the mouth of the balloon with a handful of confetti or small candies.

What You Do:
1. Blow up your thick latex balloon about two-thirds of the way full and tie it closed.
2. Find the thickest part of the balloon (about a half inch away from the knot) and stick the skewer very carefully into the area near the knot.
3. Carefully push the skewer all the way through to the opposite, fat end of the balloon as shown. You should be able to gently glide the balloon all the way through and out.

Once out, puncture the balloon with the sharp skewer and watch the confetti or candies spill out, like a miniature piñata!

The Science:

The cooking oil is used to help seal the hole. The elastic nature of the latex balloon also aids in filling the hole!

Flying with Mirrors
Strap on your bicycle helmet!

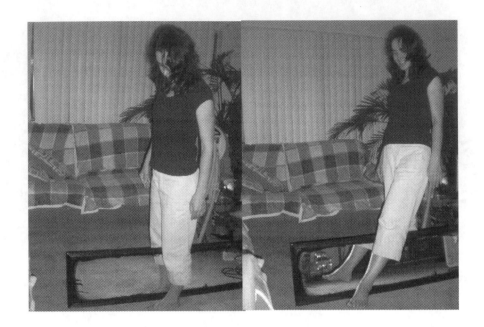

Materials:
- a wardrobe mirror (about 2 feet wide by 6 feet high)
- yourself

What You Do:

1. Simply position the mirror between your legs as shown.

2. Balance yourself whichever of your legs is behind the mirror and out of view of your audience.

3. Lift up the leg that's in front of the mirror at about a forty-five-degree angle.

4. Keeping the angle, push out your leg at least eighteen inches away from the mirror.

5. From your audience's view, you are levitating about two feet off the ground!

The Science:

The mirror gives the illusion of your two legs floating! The reflection of the one leg that's in front of the mirror gives us the appearance of two legs. Our eyes are seeing two legs, and this information is sent along the optic nerve to the brain. This is a perfect example of a classic optical illusion, whereby the brain "agrees" with the image that the eyes see!

Giant Hole in Hand

You won't believe your eyes!

Materials:

- a large mailing tube, about 17 inches long and 3 to 4 inches in diameter, or an 11-by-17-inch poster board or card stock paper
- masking tape

What You Do:

1. Obtain a mailing tube or tape together a piece of poster board or card stock paper into a cylinder-shaped tube with hole about three or four inches in diameter.

2. Hold the tube with your right hand so that its end is positioned on the right side of your outstretched left hand. Keep both eyes open as you view the tube with your right eye. The tube should be held about two inches from your right eye.

3. Look through the tube with your right eye while at the same time using your left eye to look at the place where your left hand ends and the tube begins! Do you see the hole in your hand?

The Science:

Your eyes are seeing two images at once—your hand, and the hole in the tube. By combining the images, you get the illusion of both the hole and the hand—or more precisely, a hole in your hand! Try looking at other images and see if you see a hole.

The Incredible Twisted Arm Illusion
Never give away this (science) secret!

What You Need:
- an audience
- a long-sleeved shirt
- a volunteer
- a short-sleeved shirt

Preparation and Performance:

1. You wear the long-sleeved shirt, and have your volunteer wear a short-sleeved shirt.

2. Standing next to your volunteer, put your left hand down flat in front of your body. Have your volunteer do the same as they stand to your left. (See photo A.)

3. Now secretly pick up your hand and twist it counterclockwise 360 degrees so it's back pointing the original direction again. (See photo B.)

Now ask your volunteer to follow along as you both twist your arms clockwise. (See photo C.)

What is happening? Your friend will only be able to rotate their hand a few inches, while you can rotate your hand 360 degrees!

The Science:

The principle behind this trick can also be seen during a performance of the uneven bars in gymnastics. The gymnast twists his wrist and hand so he is able to turn himself completely around! This is really an example of an optical illusion in which the eyes see the arm twisting 360 degrees, while the brain maintains that this is impossible! The long-sleeved shirt is really what is twisting 360 degrees, not your hand!

The Powerful Paper Clip
This will fool even the sharpest!

Materials and Preparation:

- a paper clip
- a glass of water three-quarters of the way full
- a friend
- any magnet, secretly placed in your pocket

What You Do:

Ask your friend to drop the paper clip into the cup of water.

Now challenge your friend to get the paper clip out of the water without touching the paper clip, the glass, or the water!

What happens?

Let your friend struggle a bit before introducing the magnet. Now he or she should be able to remove the paper clip by placing the magnet on the outside of the cup and while moving the magnet up against the cup. The paper clip should follow the magnet until it is out of the glass of water!

Hypnotic Disc

Future vision

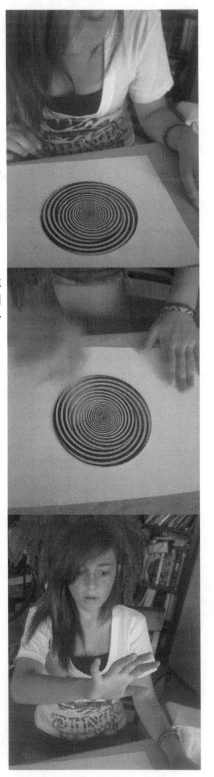

Materials:

- a hypnotic disc, obtainable from a local magic store or online

What You Do:

Spin the disc and stare at the middle nonstop for at least forty-five seconds for an unbelievable, eye-popping experience!

What is happening: everything in your range of vision will appear to swirl dizzily around you!

The Science:

The rods (the parts of your eye responsible for seeing black and white) become weary of watching the hypnotic circles and therefore begin to work less efficiently for a few seconds after staring at the disc.

Mirror Maze Race
Think backwards to win the race!

Materials:
- a few sheets of copy, printer, or colorful paper
- a pencil or colorful marker
- a mirror about 10 inches square (or a handheld mirror)

Preparation:

Draw any kind of maze with a start and a finish. The maze should be at least one-half inch wide throughout the course. The maze can be random, such as a picture, the letters of your name, or whatever you wish. You can have just one solution to the finish line, or several. You may use many colors or just one.

What You Do:

Once drawn, challenge a friend to travel through your maze using their finger. It should only take the person a minute or two to reach the finish line.

Now, add a little science magic! Place a mirror flat upright in front of the maze. Tell the maze racer to keep their eyes on the mirror during the duration of the next maze race! Picking up a pencil or marker, try going through the maze looking only at the mirror. Not so easy now, huh?

The Science:

When one looks into a mirror, the image one sees appears backwards. This illusion confuses the brain, as the eyes see a backwards message while the brain tries to unscramble it.

Ultimate Maze Race

Put a new spin on the traditional foot race!

Materials and Preparation:
- some large pieces of chalk or a chalk paint sprayer
- a large, clear area where you can draw your giant maze with your chalk or a grassy area where you can build a maze with paper cups
- two to three rectangular mirrors
- two volunteers

What You Do:

1. Draw a maze with thick, colorful lines (having various paths and dead ends). Make sure the maze is large enough so someone may run through it. Include a few starting and ending points.

2. Have your volunteers hold up the mirrors at the finish line.

3. Looking only at the mirror at all times, begin racing against the clock or against another racer who starts at a different point in the maze.

The Science:

Looking in a mirror reflects objects backwards! So, as you race, your eyes will give you a backwards message, while your brain tries to adjust and keep you on the right track in the maze.

Infinity Mirrors
Test the concept of infinity!

Materials:

- two same-sized mirrors
- a friend or volunteer

What You Do:

Face two mirrors at each other and have someone place their face in between both mirrors. He or she can see the endless reflections between the mirrors!

What is happening?

You can see the same infinity mirror effect at Disneyland's "Haunted House" attraction. All you need is the perpetual reflection of mirrors and some light, so the image can bounce back and forth and back and forth and …

Walking on the Ceiling
No suction cups required!

Materials:
- a handheld mirror at least 5 inches square

What You Do:

Hold a handheld mirror against one side of your body directed toward the ceiling. Simply glance down as you walk across the room. Does it feel weird?

What is happening?

It appears that the ceiling is under your feet as you go strolling along. The ceiling is reflected in the mirror, so the illusion makes it seem as if your feet are on the ceiling! Since you are looking down, your brain is confused and does not process the fact that the ceiling is really above you!

Self-Portrait Illusion

Become your own illusion

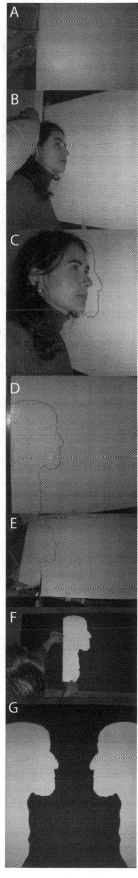

Materials and Preparation:
- a thick, black poster board at least 3 feet by 4 feet
- two white poster boards
- a flashlight
- scissors
- some wall space
- a friend

What You Do:

1. Holding the two white poster boards as one, tape them onto the wall so you can fit the side of your head against the middle section of the poster boards. (See photo A.)

2. Have a friend hold a flashlight illuminating a shadow portrait of your profile.

3. Have your friend draw the outline of your silhouette created by the flashlight. (See photo B and C) Make sure to complete the outline both above and below your head as well.

4. Remove the two white boards from the wall.

5. Cut out the entire drawing on **both** white poster boards. (See photos E and F.)

6. Place both cutout portraits face to face about ten inches apart onto the black poster board and glue them into place. (See photo G)

Staring at the science art you have just created, you should see your two portrait profiles or, if you look at it another way, a picture of a vase in the middle!

The Science:

This optical illusion demonstrates the challenge the brain has when it tries to process two images at once. The eyes send the images of the portraits and the vase simultaneously down the optic nerve. The brain can only understand one vision at a time, explaining the flip-flopping of vases versus faces!

Haunted Family Art Gallery
Scare yourself silly with this family science art activity.

Materials:
- a couple of magazines
- scissors
- a glue stick or some clear glue
- three to four sheets of card stock paper

What You Do:

1. Finds several colorful magazine photographs of people with big smiles and expressive eyes. (See photo A.)

2. Draw rectangles around the eyes and mouths. (See photo B.)

3. Carefully and precisely cut out the eyes and mouths as shown in photo C.

4. Now, cut out the pages with the faces (minus the eyes and mouths), turn the pages upside down, and glue them onto the card stock as in photo D.

5. Glue the eyes and mouths **right side up** onto the upside-down pictures in the holes from which you cut them as shown in E.

Challenge a friend to see if there is anything wrong with the picture, besides the obvious fact that the smiling person is upside down. (See photo F.)

The Science:

The brain cannot process anything upside down, and the model looks as if an alien monster has invaded her body! Now that's what I call fright gallery!

Interesting fact: We are born seeing upside down. We still see the world upside down, but our brains flip the world over so we may go about our daily lives!

Floating Bread

Please pass the bread!

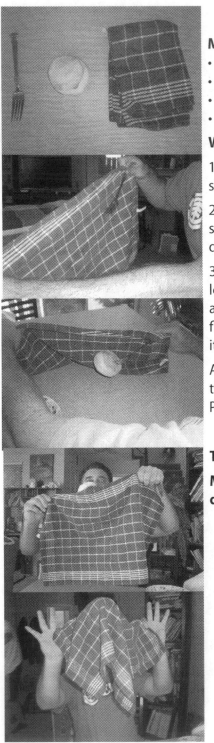

Materials:
- a large, dark cloth napkin
- a medium-sized bread roll
- a strong metal fork
- an audience

What You Do:

1. Hold the handle side of a fork under the napkin as shown.

2. Show the bread roll to the audience and then cover it so you can stick the fork into it (but do not show that you are doing so!).

3. Say something along the lines of, "Seems like there's a lot of yeast in bread these days," just as you move the fork and napkin as shown, giving the illusion that the bread is floating! (The fork must move hidden under the napkin. Hold it easily with your thumb and pointing finger.)

Allow the bread to peek over the top of the napkin. Make sure this move and all moves are done smoothly and naturally. Practice this in front of the mirror at before showing anyone!

The Science:

Magic? Maybe. To be sure, it's a visual illusion of a gravity-defying object!

Rope Through Friends
An impossible solid-through-solid penetration!

Materials and Preparation:
- two colorful 7- to 10-foot ropes of equal length
- some thread
- two to four kids

Tie a strong thread to the ropes as shown in photo A. Hold the two ropes carefully so no one sees the threaded connection.

What You Do:

1. Ask two to three volunteers to stand shoulder to shoulder and face the audience.

2. Secretly position the ropes as shown in photo B and call for another volunteer to help hold the ropes behind the kids' backs as shown in photo C.

3. Both the magician (you) and the last volunteer should take one end of the ropes you are each holding and bring them around in front to securely tie the two or three kids in place as seen in photo D.

4. On the count of three, you, the magician, and your third volunteer should pull your ropes.

The thread will break, making it appear that the ropes have mysteriously passed through the children like magic! (See photo E.)

The Science:

This is a fantastic trick that challenges the notion of solid penetrating solid! We learn early on through everyday experiences solid objects cannot penetrate other solid objects. As a result, this trick is actually an optical illusion: the rope only appears to penetrate the volunteer!

Ancient Mummy Illusion
Can solid matter disappear?

Materials:

- an extra-large blanket or dark sheet, at least 7 feet long and as tall as your volunteers
- three people, all about the same size
- an exit door behind your blanket or sheet

What You Do:

1. Hold one end of the blanket or sheet as an "accomplice" holds the opposite end as in photo A. Hold the blanket or sheet taut between the two of you.

2. In the meantime, have a third person hidden behind the blanket or sheet. (See photo B.)

3. Have your accomplice start to wrap himself in the blanket or sheet. At the same time, have the hidden person grab the edge of the blanket next to your accomplice's hand. The hidden person's hand should appear to replace the accomplice's hand. See photo C. (This is accomplished as the accomplice is out of sight.)

As the previously hidden friend wraps himself up like a mummy (see photos D and E), the accomplice runs out of the door or hides out of sight (photo F). You can then unwrap the mummy, revealing the magic transportation of people! (See photo G.)

The Science:

Of course, matter—anything that has weight and takes up space—cannot disappear. It can only change form—i.e., from a liquid like water into a steamy gas. Yet with this illusion, it seems like your friend has vanished into thin air, replaced by someone who appeared from nowhere.

Ghostly Touch
A friendly shout-out to a ghost!

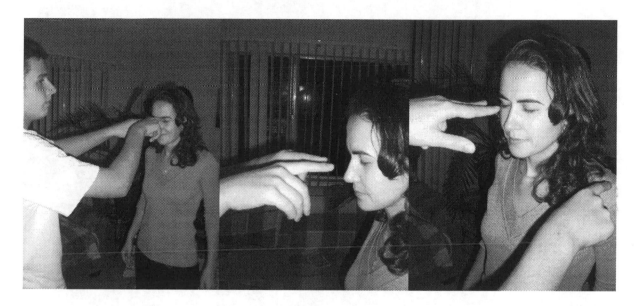

Materials:
- a reliable volunteer
- your two hands

What You Do:

1. Ask your volunteer if they believe in ghosts. Whatever the response, let them know you will conjure up a friendly apparition!

2. Hold both of your hands about five inches away from the volunteer's open eyes.

3. Point both index fingers toward your volunteer's eyes.

4. Now ask the person to close both eyes.

5. As soon as their eyes close, move your right hand away and spread the first and second fingers of your left hand as shown.

6. Lightly touch the volunteer's eyelids with these two fingers, reminding them to keep their eyes closed the entire time or else the ghost will be scared off.

7. They will feel the sensations on both their eyelids and will assume you are using both of your hands to touch them.

8. Call out your friendly ghost and tap the volunteer on their right shoulder with your free right hand.

Quickly bring both your hands back into their original positions, and when the person opens their eyes, they too will believe in ghosts!

The Science:

The perception is that the magician is using three fingers from **two hands**, and the brain processes this information incorrectly, which adds to the illusion. This self-explanatory illusion is highly effective, fun, and puzzles even the know-it-alls!

Capture a Ghost

You will have them believing in ghosts!

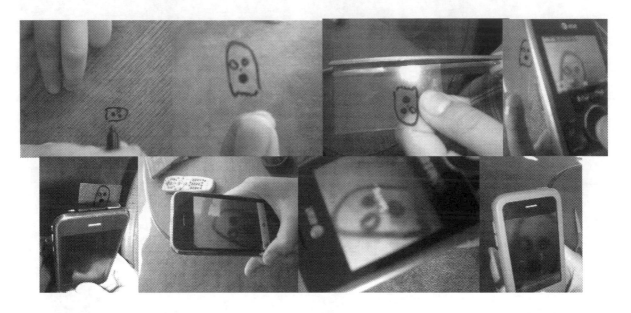

Materials:
- a cell phone with a camera feature, or any digital camera
- some plastic laminate, available at print shops
- a black Sharpie pen

Preparation:

Draw a small "ghostly figure" on your clear plastic sheet. Cut out the plastic so it measures about half an inch by one inch.

What You Do:

Using one hand to hold the camera and the other to hold the laminated ghost (secretly), pass the ghostly drawing quickly in front of your cell phone camera lens and take a picture. With practice, you will have your observer truly believing in ghosts!

Tip: You may want to come up with a wonderful ghost story and see if you can capture the ghost that haunts your area!

The Science: Scientists often are looking for evidence to support their hypotheses, or "smart guesses." The lack of supportive evidence that ghosts are real means that their existence is nothing but science fiction—at least, as far as we know!

CHAPTER 8: EXTREME NATURE

Rainbow Fishing For Ice!
"Reel" in the excitement!

Materials and Preparation:
- two 12-inch-long cotton strings
- dyed ice cubes (prepare the day before in ice an tray with different food coloring added to each space)
- a container of salt
- a wide, medium-sized glass (a plastic glass will work, too)
- a separate glass filled two-thirds of the way with cold water (See photo A.)

Time for some ice fishing! What will you catch? A swordfish? Shark? Angel fish? Mermaid? Let your imagination run wild!

What You Do:
1. Place your "fishing pole" string in an S shape over the ice cubes with about three to four inches of string hanging over the side. (See photo B.)
2. Now, very quickly, add about five to seven pinches of salt right on top of all parts of the string that are in contact with the ice cubes. (See photo C.)
3. Count fifteen seconds. Then, lift up on the free end of the string and voila! You have just caught several ice fish! (See photos D and E.)

Grab a new, clean string and repeat!

The Science:

As the ice begins to melt, the salt reacts by helping the string "stick" to the ice. Salt lowers the freezing point of water.

Sun Shadows
The sixty-five thousand mile per hour experiment!

Materials:
- blue, red, and green colored chalk
- a friend
- the sun
- a stretch of sidewalk

What You Do:

1. Find a bright, open area. Ask each participant to take turns as a 'statutes" as you carefully draw the outline of their shadow with chalk created by sunlight.

2. Write down the time and your friend's name next to the shadow sketch.

3. Come back about thirty minutes later and have your friend stand in the same position as before, with his or her feet inside the sketched outline.

4. Draw the new shadow with a different color of chalk. Write down the new time.

5. Return one or two hours later and draw a third shadow with the same statue pose in another different color of chalk.

The Science:

Your controlled experiment demonstrates the movement of the earth as it rotates around the sun, evidenced by the movement of the shadows. Shadows grow and shrink faster in the mid morning and mid afternoon and slower around noon, when the sun is directly above! Believe it or not, we humans travel 65,000 miles per hour as we are spun around in our earthly orbit!

Orbiting House

Hold on!

Materials:
- you
- your house
- the sun

What You Do:

1. Position yourself with your house between you and the setting sun.

2. You should be in an elevated place if possible, about twenty to forty yards from your house. The sun should appear to be a few inches above your house.

3. Stare only at the top of your house where the sun is setting. Never look directly at the sun itself!

4. As you focus your view on the house, it will appear to move ever so slowly as the sun sets behind it!

The Science:

Since the earth is what's moving, not the sun, you are truly watching your house move!

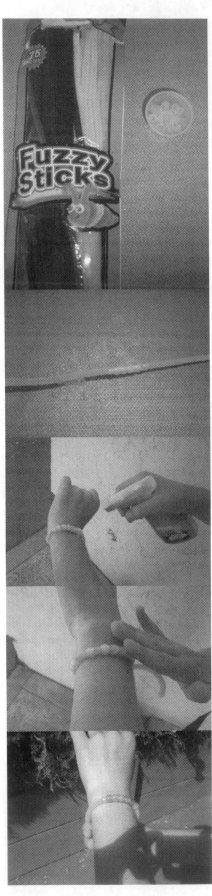

Ultraviolet Sun Beads

Science you can wear!

Materials:
- ultraviolet color-changing beads, available from a science or teacher supply store
- two types of sun block—one SPF 15 and another SPF 40 or higher
- lanyard or soft material used for making bracelets

What You Do:

1. Inside and away from any sunlight, assemble a bracelet with a handful of ultraviolet light beads.

2. Assemble a second bracelet, but cover these beads thoroughly with sun block.

3. Go to a window or outside and expose both sets of beads to direct sunlight. Observe any changes.

4. Next, go outside to an area with shade and try it again.

The Science:

Ultraviolet light is an invisible light that comes through holes in the ozone layer. UV light can be harmful to plants and animals, even humans. The untreated beads detect the invisible light and change from clear beads to a rainbow of colors. What happened when you coated your beads with sun block at SPF 15? How about with sun block at SPF 40 or higher?

Attack of the Venus Flytrap
Keep a safe distance from these meat eaters!

Materials and Preparation:
- Venus flytrap
- something to catch bugs in, such as a jar
- small, sharp scissors
- bugs (you can buy crickets or find flies, dead or alive!)
- toothpicks

What You Do:

1. Buy or find your own bugs.

2. Stab a bug with a toothpick. (Living bugs are better!)

3. Place the bug deep inside the mouth of one of your pet flytraps.

4. Jiggle your bug around inside the mouth until you trigger the mouth to close.

5. Remove the toothpick slowly so that your bug stays inside the trap!

6. Repeat the above steps for the number of open mouths present.

7. Cutout the mouths and look inside them.

8. Remove the flytrap from soil and observe its roots.

9. Dissect the remaining parts of the flytrap.

The Science:

Venus flytraps are carnivorous, which means they attract, kill, and digest living creatures in the animal kingdom. This includes flies, crickets, and tiny aquatic animals. The trap emits a chemical that aids in digestion after the trigger hairs close around its prey. Venus flytraps are found in North and South Carolina in humid, wet, and sunny bogs. Since the soil surrounding the trap lacks nitrogen, it must find prey that is rich in this nutrient.

Venus flytraps can live for years in the ideal climate. At home, your pet may only live a few months and can quickly turn black and die. Try keeping the plant in a warm, moist area, and have plenty of insects on hand for midnight feedings! Remember, you too have nitrogen nutrients your flytrap craves!

Mysterious Sea Creature Dissection Made Simple
A great first dissection to stimulate young scientists.

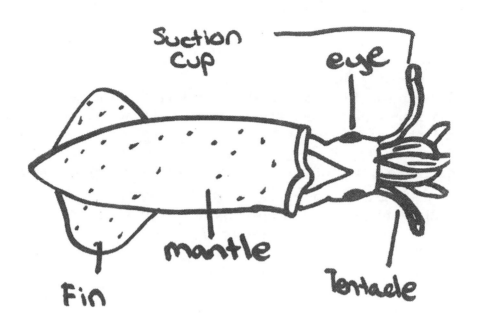

Materials:
- frozen squid, available at your local seafood market
- scissors
- a strong plastic plate

What You Do:

1. Examine the outside of your squid for the mantle (main body), the two fins, two eyes, tentacles, and beak, which is found between the tentacles.

2. Count how many tentacles your squid has and how many of them have suction cups on their ends.

3. Using your hands, pull out the sea creature's beak, which it uses to bite. The white brains are connected and should be attached to the beak as you remove both together!

4. Dissect the tentacles (cut them out for closer examination).

5. Using your scissors, dissect through the squid starting at the mouth where the beak used to be, slicing along the length of the mysterious sea creature. While cutting, be careful not to disturb its many internal organs.

6. Locate one to three of the squid's pinkish red hearts. One is located near its fins, and the other two are located closer to the center of the creature. (Most students find one or two of the three. Usually the hearts are the size of the tip of a pin; rarely they can be as large as a dime.)

7. Locate and dissect the squid's white, glistening stomach, which is used for digestion.

8. Look for its long, pale tan esophagus, where food travels down on its journey to the stomach.

9. Pull out the squid's pen (try to find it on your own) and locate the black ink sac. Dissect both and press the pen into the ink sack. Write your name using the pen and ink!

10. Dissect the fins, brown liver, and feathery white gills.

11. Dissect the eyes. Feel the hard, round lens!

- Amazing squid facts:
- Squid eat other squid, fish, crabs, and shrimp.
- Squid defend themselves by shooting a cloud of ink at their enemies.
- Squid can bite with their beaks, fly through the air, and swim very quickly through jet propulsion.
- A squid can camouflage itself against the sea's backdrop to hide from predators.
- Squid have three hearts, which aid with their tremendous speed and agility.

The squid does not have a backbone, but rather a "pen" that provides the support for its body and holds ink. Giant squid live in very deep parts of the oceans.

Collapsing Bottle of Air
A matter of air!

Materials:

- ice
- hot water
- a bucket or cooler filled two-thirds of the way with ice and cold water
- an empty two-liter bottle

What You Do:

1. Completely fill the two-liter bottle with very warm or hot water.

2. Empty the hot water out and seal the top closed.

Quickly place your sealed, empty bottle into the bucket or cooler of ice and water. Your bottle should collapse!

The Science:

The expanding very warm air is cooled by the ice and water and condenses inside the bottle. Also, surrounding air pressure pushes against the bottle, helping it collapse!

Party-Sized Pop
Big chance of showers!

Materials:
- Multi-gallon sized Ziploc bag
- a gallon of vinegar
- two 24-ounce boxes of baking soda

What You Do:

Fill the super large Ziploc bag with a full gallon of vinegar.

2. Quickly add both boxes of baking soda and quickly seal the bag.

3. You will watch the bag inflate with invisible CO_2 gas.

Shake it up to create as much gas as possible. Lay your gas sandwich on a clear, flat, grassy area. If it does not pop on its own, you may choose to jump on the inflated bag with both feet.

The Science:

The base (baking soda) and the acid (vinegar) together create CO_2 gas, which expands gas and leads to a party-sized pop!

1.

Enormous Volcano to Go!

Go green with this giant, reusable volcano maker!

Materials and Preparation:

- an extra, extra large Ziploc bag
- five boxes of baking soda
- 1/2 cup of Dawn or Joy dish soap
- one bottle of food coloring, any color
- 2 gallons of water
- 4 gallons of acetic acid (vinegar)
- a camera—you just don't want to miss this!
- a place you can perform this erupting experiment that will not harm Mom's bed of flowers!

What You Do:

1. Pour all of the baking soda, soap, and food coloring into the dry, empty bucket.

2. Pour in the two gallons of water.

3. Now for the chemical reaction, quickly pour in all of the vinegar, and either stand back or hold the bucket and feel the carbon dioxide gas bubbles erupt all over you!

The Science:

The acid (vinegar) and the base (baking soda) reacted, causing an eruption of carbon dioxide, soap, and coloring. It is very safe, even if the gas bubbles flow all over you! Wash your clothes in cold water to remove all chemicals safely!

Rock Balancing in Your Backyard
Create a natural architectural wonder in your own yard!

Materials:
- a good granite rock for use as a base stone, with a crease where you can place a pointy rock into later
- several pebbles
- several medium-size rocks with points and crevices
- a pointy rock with a flat base and small crevices
- some smaller rocks for the top

What You Do:

1. Balance our large granite rock by placing small pebbles underneath it.

2. Gently place the pointy, larger rock into a crevice of the base rock and move it back and forth until it balances via its center of gravity. This may take five or more minutes!

3. Carefully continue to add rocks on top, one at a time, as high as you can balance!

The Science:

An area known as the center of gravity is your friend for this experiment. An object's center of gravity is basically a point in which the object is perfectly balanced and should not tip over easily. An easy way to understand this concept is to stand like a statue and have someone lightly push you to one side. If you do not adjust yourself, you will fall over, because you are no longer balanced on your center of gravity.

Catch a Falling Star
Start a meteorite collection!

Materials and Preparation:
- a 5-by-5-inch piece of thin cardboard (like from a shoe box)
- a 20-inch length of string
- strong magnet tape
- scissors

What You Do:

1. Assemble your falling star (meteorite) "catcher" by taping a magnet on the bottom of the cardboard.

2. Find an area of soft dirt at least five feet long.

3. Walk along so that your catcher surfs just about a quarter of an inch from the surface of the soft ground. Be sure to walk very slowly.

4. Once you have surfed the catcher over your area for a few minutes, reel up the string slowly and look at the bottom of your contraption. Did any little round dark or silver colored metallic meteorites stick to the bottom of your cardboard?

The Science:

Meteorites are meteors that fall from the sky and look like shooting stars at night; they contain metal and will stick well to your magnet. Other metallic objects like cans may also stick to your magnet, so carefully remove those objects from your newfound space treasures! Be persistent! You may need to surf a large area to find even one or two meteorites! It is estimated that if you spend just one hour outside, chances are you will be hit by a meteorite in that time frame, however tiny it may be in size.

Black Light Painting

Create colorful works of lighted-color science art

Materials:
- paint with ultraviolet light sensitivity (such as the ones found in UV paints at Spencer's Stores)
- paper
- paintbrushes
- a UV-detecting light

Note: Be sure to use paint containing UV properties. Design your picture as you would when using any other paint. Use a black light to illuminate your painting. The UV light contained in the paints will light up your masterpiece!

What You Do:

1. Paint your special UV-detecting black light paint on your hands, arms, etc., to turn yourself into a living art masterpiece!

2. Paint a starry sky scene using the lightest color that you have available on a large black poster board and hang it over your bed at night so you can fall asleep looking at the stars!

3. Paint lines as in the "Parallel World" experiment found elsewhere in this book. Paint a spiral or other optical illusion!

4. Paint freestyle—the possibilities are endless!

The Science:

The invisible light spectrum includes gamma rays, microwaves, x-rays, radio waves, and ultraviolet rays. Ultraviolet rays are just outside of the visible light spectrum, which includes the rainbow of colors that we can see. UV rays can be made visible by a black light and can be dangerous to humans. Sun block is geared to protect us from those harmful UV rays emitted from the sun!

Bubble Mania

Concoct a fantastic bubble formula!

Materials and Preparation:

- two 5-gallon buckets, each filled with about 3 gallons of warm water
- two bottles of corn syrup
- a small bottle of food coloring
- two 16-ounce bottles of Dawn or Joy brand dish soap

1. Mix one bottle each of corn syrup and dish soap into one of the buckets.

2. Add a few drops of food coloring to that bucket if desired. Then, with clean hands, mix the chemicals together for about thirty seconds.

3. Do the same with the other bucket.

Prepare your bubble making tools:

1. Cut two to three inches off the tops of a few Dixie cups and save them for making bubbles.

2. Tie a string through two straws to use to dip into bubble formula.

3. Use masking tape to bind together about a half a dozen same-sized straws to use later as a bubble blower.

What You Do:

Dip your bubble tools into the buckets and begin blowing through them to make bubbles. Or, pour the bubble formula into a cake pan and use a large circle wand to create large, long bubbles. You may even want to make a super large batch of bubble formula and fill a child's small plastic wading pool.

Go Extreme: Bubble Party!

Trap friends inside giant bubbles!

The instructions are the same as above except:

Once you have formulated your bubble solution, pour it all into a small wading pool. Next, drop in a large hula hoop. Have three or four volunteers stand in the pool and inside the hula hoop with goggles on. Lift the hula hoop over all the volunteers and try to capture them all inside your humongous, rainbow bubble! This may take five or more passes of the hula hoop until your bubble forms!

The Science:

The corn syrup helps hold the bubbles together longer than if you used only soap. Dust particles, heat, and wind can break your bubbles. The corn syrup makes the bubbles more elastic and stronger. The rainbow color you may see in the bubbles happens when the white light from the sun splits into the color spectrum: red, orange, yellow, green, blue, indigo, and violet!

Help save the earth: Try cutting out large squares from used cardboard to use in place of the plastic hula hoop!

Geode Crystal Creations
Create beautiful crystal keepsakes for your room!

Materials and Preparation:
- one egg
- Epsom salts or natural sugar crystals (do not use processed white sugar)
- purple, blue, green, or red food coloring
- 1 cup of water in a plastic bowl

What You Do:
1. Crack an eggshell in half and remove the egg. Carefully clean out the remaining egg from the shell halves.
2. Mix about half a cup of Epsom salts or natural sugar crystals into your bowl of water.
3. Carefully scoop out your mixture and fill your eggshells about one-third of the way full of crystal solution.
4. Place the eggshells undisturbed and check on your crystals every few hours or so.
5. Observe and record your findings.

The Science:

Crystals are found in nature and include minerals, such as diamonds, snowflakes, sugar, salt, and others. No two crystals are identical. Real mineral geode crystals are formed inside the earth when very hot magma cools relatively quickly, forming such crystals as purple amethyst and quartz.

CHAPTER 9: EDIBLE DELIGHTS

Chocolate in a Minute!

Chocolate + fast = yummy!

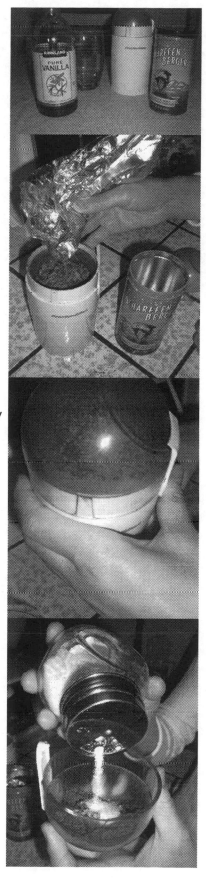

Materials:

- an electric coffee grinder
- cocoa beans, available at fancy supermarkets
- 2 tablespoons of sugar
- 1 teaspoon of vanilla extract
- 1 tablespoon of butter

What You Do:

1. Grind up the cocoa beans in your coffee grinder.

2. Place the cocoa in a microwave-safe glass bowl.

3. Add the sugar, butter, and vanilla extract to the bowl.

4. Place the bowl in the microwave for twenty seconds.

5. Remove, stir, and return to the microwave for twenty additional seconds.

6. Enjoy your fresh chocolate confection!

The Science:

Cocoa beans come from the cocoa tree, found in large abundance in South America and other parts of the world. It takes up to seven years for the cocoa beans to be ready for harvesting and then five to seven days to be fully processed into the edible chocolate you buy from a store!

The cocoa butter contained in the bean is what gives it its delicious flavor. The butter also helps emulsify, or solidify, the chocolate. The extra butter you added helps the chocolate become creamier!

Candy Clay
Science never tasted so good!

Materials and Preparation
- 3 cups of powder sugar
- 1/4 cup of light corn syrup
- 1/2 teaspoon of salt
- 1/2 stick of low-fat margarine (softened)
- 1 teaspoon of vanilla extract
- four or more food colorings
- a large bowl
- a mixing spoon
- Four small bowls
- spoons

What You Do:

1. Wash your hands.

2. Place three cups of powdered sugar, a quarter cup of corn syrup, half a teaspoon of salt, half a stick of softened margarine, and one teaspoon of vanilla extract into a large bowl.

3. Mix all the ingredients together until not sticky. You may need to add a bit more powdered sugar if the mixture is still sticky to the touch.

4. Divide the dough into four equal-sized balls and put them in different bowls.

5. Add a few drops of food coloring to each bowl.

6. Using a spoon, mix the coloring into each ball of dough.

7. Now sculpt your most inventive creations out of the candy clay. Your candy clay structures turn into candy rock, so eat them quickly or save them as sculptured keepsakes!

The Science:

Each chemical ingredient mixed together creates a new formula in food chemistry. Try adding your own flavors to your own taste!

Burger and Fries for Dessert!

An experiment that "rises" to the occasion!

Materials and Preparation:

- Bake three 7- to 9-inch yellow round cakes from a box recipe, or purchase them pre-made at a grocery store
- Bake one 7-inch square yellow cake, or buy one from the store pre-made
- chocolate frosting
- shredded coconut, dyed green
- yellow, red, and white frosting in tubes
- a safe knife
- a spoon
- red and green gumdrops or M&M's (optional)
- crispy rice cereal (optional)

What You Do:

1. Place one of your round yellow cakes on a plate. This is the bottom bun for your burger.

2. Squeeze some white frosting on your bun. This is your mayonnaise.

3. Sprinkle the green coconut on top of the mayonnaise. This is your lettuce.

4. Place a second round cake on top. This is your burger.

5. Frost the top and sides of the burger with chocolate frosting.

6. For pickles and tomatoes, press the green and red gumdrops or M&M's into the top of the burger.

7. Squeeze some red frosting on the sides of the cake. This is the ketchup oozing out of your burger. Do the same with the yellow frosting for mustard.

8. Next, place the final round cake on top of the burger. This is your top bun. Sprinkle some crispy rice cereal on top for the sesame seeds.

9. Your burger is complete! To make the French fries, cut your square cake into long pieces. Pile your fries on your plate next to the burger and add some red frosting on top as ketchup.

The Science:

Yeast, a tiny member of the fungus kingdom, is a key ingredient in baking cakes and bread. The yeast, which is alive, eats the sugar, releasing carbon dioxide gas, which gives rise to the cakes you are now enjoying! In nature, yeast aids in the decomposition of dead animals, and it is also used as a medicine to kill deadly bacteria!

Whipped Cream Painting
Create giant, edible science art!

Materials and Preparation:
- a can of real whipped cream
- four colors of food coloring
- card stock poster paper
- paintbrushes
- bowls to hold whipped cream paint

1. Fill five bowls full of whipped cream.

2. Add food coloring to each and mix in the colors to create at least five different colored paints.

3. Place the bowls with the various colored whipped creams in a freezer for five to ten minutes.

What You Do:

1. Remove all bowls from the freezer and start to paint onto your card stock poster board.

2. Eat your edible science as you go along or put your edible artwork back in the freezer to save for later!

The Science:

Whipped cream consists of heavy cream (fat) and is filled with air. The fat and sugar give whipped cream its delicious taste! Try spraying some whipped cream in a bowl and placing it on your table. Check on it in a few hours, and it will have shrunken in size! The reason? The air pumped inside the whipped cream has escaped! Ice cream also shrinks, since it, too, is pumped full of air!

Monster Marshmallows
Watch your monsters "blow up!"

Materials:
- Handful of large marshmallows
- small marshmallows
- an assortment of candies, such as M&M's, Nerds, Jelly Bellies, thin licorice, and chocolate graham crackers
- toothpicks
- a small plate

What You Do:

1. Assemble your delicious supplies into a unique monster of your creation, using toothpicks to hold it together.

2. Rest your monster on top of the chocolate graham cracker on the plate.

3. Place your creation in the microwave.

4. Cook on high power for fifteen to twenty seconds.

5. Watch the magic through the microwave's window.

Go Extreme: Monster S'more

Place your edible creature on a Hershey's chocolate bar and that's on top of a graham cracker to create a monster s'more!

What is happening?

Your marshmallow monster is blowing up like a balloon! Marshmallows are full of air, and those gasses expand when heated by a microwave. Remove the toothpicks, let your creature cool, and then eat it!

Shake-and-Make Martian Ice Cream
An all-time favorite!

Materials and Preparation:
- two quart-sized Hefty brand plastic zipper bags
- two gallon-sized Hefty brand zipper bags
- warm gloves
- a metal spoon
- bowls or cups to serve it
- 5 cups of heavy cream or half and half
- 1 cup of sugar
- 1 tablespoon of real vanilla extract
- additional flavorings, such as chocolate chips, gummy candies, and fruit, to your personal taste
- 4 cups of ice
- 1 cup of rock salt
- two or three friends to help you shake and make delicious ice cream

What You Do:
1. Fill a one-quart Hefty zipper bag with the cream, sugar, vanilla extract, and additional flavors or add-ins.

2. Zip the filled bag closed, making sure there isn't an air pocket inside.

3. Fit this filled bag into the second, empty one-quart bag.

4. Zip up this second bag (containing the zipped first bag full of ingredients) without any air pocket. You now have double-zipped one-quart bags. (You use double bags in case one bag tears. The second bag will prevent the ingredients from leaking out.)

5. Lay your double-zipped bags in one of your empty one-gallon zipper bags.

6. Add the one cup of rock salt on top of your one-quart double bag.

7. Now fill the remainder of the one-gallon bag with four cups of ice.

8. Zip this one-gallon zipper bag, making sure to avoid any air pocket.

9. Place this filled and closed gallon zipper bag into your remaining empty gallon zipper bag and zip the second bag closed without any air pocket.

10. Wearing a pair of mittens or gloves, begin shaking the set of four bags vigorously.

The ice cream should be ready after you and your group has taken turns shaking continuously for about twenty to twenty-five minutes!

The Science:

Rock salt helps lower the freezing point of water, in essence, bringing the temperature inside the insulated bags at about 10 to 25 degrees Fahrenheit—far colder than water's normal freezing point of 32 degrees.

Try making sorbet! Substitute blended fruit for cream and eliminate the vanilla extract!

Go Extreme: Martian Ice Cream:

Add food coloring, Pop Rocks candies, a cup of soda, some gummy worms, etc., to the recipe above—or add your own "out of this world" ingredients on your way to your own inventive frozen delight!

Delicious Insects
Build a bug workshop!

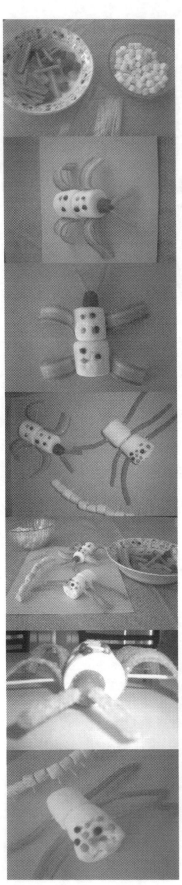

Materials:
- many types of marshmallows—large and small, white and colorful, fruit-flavored ones
- gum drops (Dots brand works very well, Juicy Fruit gum drops are also adequate)
- grapes of all sizes
- other candies: Nerds, Fruit Roll-Ups, strawberries, banana and apple slices, sour candy straws, chocolate chips, hard candies, and jelly beans
- toothpicks

What You Do:

1. Imagine you are making an insect. Make a mental picture of your bug.

2. Choose the supplies you will need to build your bug. Be creative.

3. Draw your model insect here with its real body parts marked correctly:

4. Assemble your insect by connecting your delicious supplies with rounded toothpicks.

5. Be flexible. Your first idea may be replaced by a better one. When building your bug, be careful not to poke yourself. Tip: sticky marshmallows can be the "glue" to help hold your insect together.

6. Science challenge: name off all of your insect's body parts before eating it.

7. More fun: have an insect contest. Winners may include: most beautiful insect, most dangerous, silliest insect, and so on! Try to guess the name of the insect your friend has created.

Go Extreme: 3-D Creepy Crawlers

Try creating a 3-D model insect. Try building an insect with your eyes closed! Build a bug resembling an actual photo of your favorite insect! Discover more about your favorite insect on the Web—no pun intended!

Insect Science and Fun Facts

* All insects have three main body parts: head, thorax (middle), and abdomen.

*Butterflies, ants, beetles, dragonflies, bees, moths, the walking stick insect, and ladybugs are all insects. Can you name other insects?

*80 percent of all animals are insects!

*Insects breathe through tiny holes found throughout their bodies. The holes are called spiracles!

*Some insects have spots, wings, stingers, wild colors, compound eyes, and other features!

*Insects have evolved and survived over millions of years.

*Insects can be found in almost all areas of the world.

*Only the coldest or most dry places are free of insects!

Go Extreme Cuisine!: Real, Edible Bugs

Makes the notion of eating broccoli sound delicious!

Materials:

- a box of BBQ, cheddar cheese, or Mexican spice Larvets (worms!), available through hotlix.com

The Science:

Of course, these tasty worms are not insects—no legs, for one! Many people in Africa and Mexico eat worms, and in fact, almost all animals are edible. (Yes, worms are in the animal kingdom.) Worms are high in protein and are low fat! And some say, when properly cooked, they taste like chicken! Cluck!

Edible Masterpiece
Too beautiful to eat, too delicious not to!

Materials and Preparation:
- white card stock 8 1/2 inches by 11 inches. You may substitute this with edible rice paper, so you may eat your masterpiece, paper and all!
- a bottle of corn syrup
- several kinds of candies to stick onto your masterpiece
- four colors of food coloring
- four or five clean paintbrushes
- cups

What You Do:

1. Add different colors of food coloring into different cups with corn syrup, which you will use to paint on your card stock sheet.

2. Paint a scene; for example, you can paint a yellow sun, a blue sky, and a dark green ocean using colorful corn syrup paint.

3. Now stick your various candies to the picture to complete your scene.

4. Hang your masterpiece on the wall or lick it and eat! Perfectly delicious art!

The Science:

The corn syrup, a type of sugar, is thick and therefore has a high viscosity (that is, it's a liquid that resists flow, even from the pull of gravity!). Corn syrup's high viscosity means that it does not drip, and so it makes for a perfect edible art background!

Jolly Rancher Candy Soda

Discover the food chemist inside of you!

Materials and Preparation:

- seven to ten pieces of hard Jolly Rancher candy
- 3 to 4 ounces of hot water in a large cup
- 1 to 2 ounces of sour powder or spray candy
- a small bottle of chilled sparkling or carbonated water

What You Do:

1. Drop your Jolly Rancher candies into the cup of very hot water and allow them to dissolve.

2. Mix in any candy remaining in the bottom of the cup.

3. Once the mixture has cooled, add your sour powder or spray candies and mix for about a minute.

4. Finally, open and pour your carbonated water into your mixture and drink!

Go Extreme: Soda Creations

Find your own tasty ingredients and create a unique recipe soda!

Suggestions: add melted gummy candies or fruit extracts, such as orange or lemon. Mix in soda flavors. Fortify your drink with vitamin C. Think of your own!

The Science:

The hot water melted the candies, and the dissolved flavors got mixed with the other ingredients to create your own inventive soda! You can now call yourself an amateur "flavor chemist." To your health!

Great White Shark Alert!
Bite back!

Materials and Preparation:
- a bowl or bucket filled with water
- twenty or more blue and white shark candies, available at candy stores
- a ruler

What You Do:

1. Measure the lengths of the gummy shark candies.

2. Drop them all into the bucket of water.

3. Observe and measure the sharks every few hours.

4. Try not to have nightmares.

5. Remember to bite back!

The Science:

The protein, starch, and glucose in the gummy sharks help absorb water and explain how the elastic candies swell to super size. Eventually, the water will dissolve the "giants," allowing you to have a peaceful night's sleep once again!

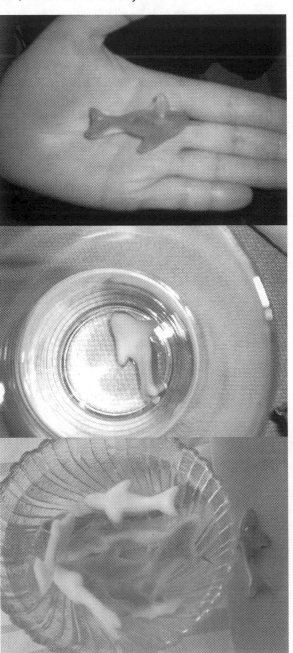

Seaweed Gummy Yummies!'
Bring the magic of the ocean into your kitchen!

Materials:

- one "Make Your Own Gummies from Scratch" kit, manufactured by Verve, Inc. and available at www.gleegum.com

What You Do:

1. Get yourself to a beach and find a piece of seaweed to adopt and take home for scientific purposes.

2. Follow the instructions listed in the gummy making kit. And remain calm—you don't have to munch on the seaweed!

The Science:

The seaweed contains a substance called carrageenan, which gels your gummy candies. Carrageenan is found in toothpastes, ice cream, and even sandwich meat!

Delicious Towering Structures
Build, learn, and eat!

Materials:
- five hundred to one thousand toothpicks
- two to four boxes of Dots gummy drops
- one to two bags of large white or multicolored marshmallows
- one bag of small multicolored marshmallows
- any other candy you can stick a toothpick into!

What You Do:

1. Start connecting your candy building materials, utilizing toothpicks as your beam connectors.

2. Use geometric shapes, such as triangles, squares, and hexagons. Heavier building materials should be close to the base of the structure to help give support. What will you build? A tall pyramid? An arch? A rectangular building? The sky is the limit!

The Science:

Real buildings require planning and blueprints, strong materials, and an understanding of math and science! Plan out what materials you will use. Will you need to use two beams (toothpicks) in connecting your candy? Can marshmallows be used to help hold (stick) some parts together, like mortar does for brick? Most likely you will rebuild as you learn what works and what causes your tall, delicious tower to come crashing down. Fire and water damage, along with poor construction, are the leading causes of structure collapse. Go Extreme: Earthquake!

Once you are satisfied with your structure, give your table a good shake to see if a mini earthquake can send your structure crashing!

Safety tip: never put toothpicks in your mouth as you begin eating your delicious structure.

Lightning in your Mouth!

Don't blink or you'll miss the action!

Materials:

- a pack of sugar-free Wintergreen Lifesavers
- a dark room with a large mirror

What You Do:

1. Make sure the bathroom or other room is pitch black.

2. Stare into mirror while chewing your handful of Life Savers Wintergreen Mints.

3. Observe the flashes of light!

The Science:

The candies are coated with an oil called methyl salicylate, which is florescent and gives off a faint light when chewed. Almost any object will spark when it is smashed. The faint light a smashed object emits is called triboluminescence.

CHAPTER 10: PARENT AND CHILD TOGETHER: CLASSIFIED SECRET SCIENCE

(Please note: all experiments in this section require adult participation and supervision!)

Liquid Nitrogen Ice Cream
Safety first! Delicious ice cream second!

Materials and Preparation:

- a stainless steel mixing bowl
- a wooden spoon
- safety glasses and safety gloves
- 5 liters of liquid nitrogen (approximately -320 degrees F) in a metal container (Check your yellow pages)
- 1 quart of heavy cream
- 1 pint of regular milk
- 1 cup of sugar
- 3 tablespoons of vanilla extract
- optional items: food coloring, chocolate chips, and flavor extracts, such as orange, banana, etc.

What You Do:

1. You **must** wear gloves and goggles. Put them on **right now**!

2. Place your cream, sugar, vanilla extract, and all other optional food items into a stainless steel bowl.

3. Carefully pour about one liter of liquid nitrogen liquid into the bowl.

4. Wait about thirty seconds and then start mixing for about fifteen seconds. (Some parts will freeze, others will remain liquid.)

5. Add another one liter or so of the liquid nitrogen gas wait thirty seconds. Then mix again for fifteen seconds.

6. Repeat step 4 three more times.

Keeping your safety items on, serve up about a half gallon of delicious gourmet science ice cream!

The Science:

Your ice cream creation is the "avenge grade" way to science heaven. The liquid nitrogen quickly freezes the fat and nonfat parts of your cream. This quick freeze method gives your dairy delight its smooth texture!

Dry Ice Soda
A natural CO_2 soda recipe!

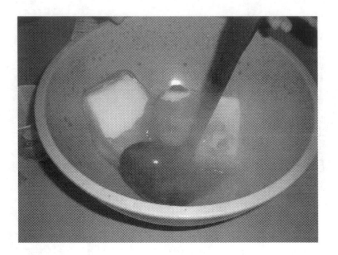

Materials and Preparation:
- 2 to 3 pounds of dry ice
- 1 gallon of fruit juice
- a large, sturdy plastic or metal bowl
- safety gloves
- a serving spoon for liquids
- Cups

What You Do:

1. With your dry ice in your bowl, simply pour the juice over the dry ice.

2. Watch the fog (evaporating CO_2 gas) travel upward! Wait thirty minutes or so and serve your science soda! Do not eat or drink the ice!

The Science:

Carbon dioxide gas will begin to warm and evaporate into the air. Some of the gas, however, will enter the juice, giving it its fizziness and creating soda pop!

Mad Science Soda

Experience the excitement of mad science soda!

Materials and Preparation:

- 2 to 3 pounds of dry ice
- safety gloves
- 1/4 cup of banana, strawberry, orange, or root beer extract
- 2 gallons of filtered water
- 1 cup of sugar
- a clean and sanitized 5-gallon ice cooler
- optional food items, such as gummy worms, pop rock candies, etc.

What You Do:

1. Wearing safety gloves and using metal tongs, place the dry ice inside your clean ice cooler.

2. Add the water.

3. Add your fruit or other extract.

4. Add the sugar.

5. Mix for two to three minutes as the sugar dissolves.

Wait five minutes or more and serve!

The Science:

Consider yourself a food chemist; you have just created a mad science soda using an evaporating gas, carbon dioxide—the same gas used to make our store-bought sodas fizz!

Ghostly Bubbles
An effervescent experience!

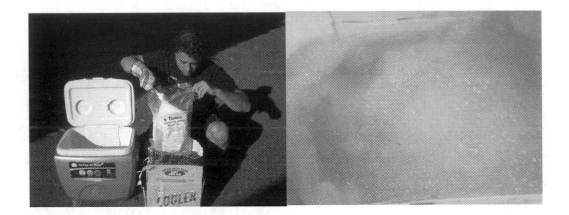

Materials:

- 2 to 3 pounds of dry ice
- 4 tablespoons of dish soap
- 2 quarts of very warm water
- a few drops of food coloring
- a small (3- to 5-gallon) ice cooler
- safety gloves

What You Do:

1. Carefully place the dry ice in the ice cooler using your safety gloves.

2. Add one quart of warm water to the dry ice.

3. Add two tablespoons of dish soap to the cooler.

4. If desired, add few drops of food coloring.

Watch ghostly bubbles form, rise, and pop in a poof of fog!

The Science:

Adding warm water speeds up the gas's natural evaporation process. As the CO_2 gas begins to evaporate into the air, soap bubbles are carried up. The soap bubbles contain some of the carbon dioxide, as evidenced in the poof of smoky fog.

Boo Bubbles
The magic of science!

Materials:
- a "Boo Bubbles" kit from www.SteveSpanglerScience.com

What You Do:

Follow the instructions to make amazing frozen bubbles. This kit is great for Halloween, chemistry experiments, or just to have fun!

The Science:

The frozen carbon dioxide gas—dry ice—eerily becomes trapped inside your bubble. Bubbles hold together well until popped by an abrasive object!

Up in Flames

Who says a dollar does not go very far these days?

Materials and Preparation:
- one crisp dollar bill
- three aluminum bowls (one filled one-third of the way with rubbing alcohol; a second one filled one-third of the way with a half rubbing alcohol, half water mixture; and one filled one-third of the way with water only)
- safety tongs
- safety glasses
- safety gloves
- a lighter or some matches

What You Do:

1. While wearing safety glasses, lower the dollar bill using your tongs into the bowl with water alone, and then light a match or lighter and bring the flame to it. Nothing happens.

2. Next, using tongs, lower the same dollar bill into the alcohol-water mixture. Then try to light it in the same fashion as in step 1. A small, bluish flame surrounds the dollar, yet the bill itself is not destroyed.

3. Now, using your tongs again, drench the dollar bill in the bowl with rubbing alcohol. Hold the bill over the bowl of water. Keeping the bill far away from yourself, others, and everything else, try to light the alcohol-soaked dollar as in the first two steps. A huge flame! Yet, the dollar remains intact!

4. Dry off the dollar. Finally, try to light the dollar bill as it is, with no liquid on it. Watch as it becomes quite apparent that money can—and does—burn!

The Science:

In the first step, the water prevents the bill from burning. In the next step, the water contains the small fire ignited by the flammable rubbing alcohol. In the third step, the flame consumes the alcohol, and the fire goes out quickly. In the final step, the dollar bill burns, as it is made from paper and other flammable chemicals.

Flaming Head
Keep a good head on your shoulders!

Materials and Preparation:
- one water balloon filled fully with water
- one water balloon filled half with air and half with water
- a long lighter
- markers
- a volunteer

What You Do:

1. Draw a picture of your friends' heads onto each of the balloons.

2. Over a sink, hold the lighter flame under the balloon that's filled with both air and water. The balloon pops, and the water spills out!

3. Have your volunteer sit in a chair.

4. Hold the balloon that's filled only with water about four feet over your unsuspecting volunteer's head and say, "Now let's get you really wet!"

Ask him to close his eyes and then light your lighter so the flame is licking the bottom of the balloon. Why isn't the balloon popping?

The Science:

The first balloon is cooled only partially, because it has little water, and therefore it pops when heated. With the second balloon, the water conducts heat away from the latex balloon. Thus, the balloon does not get hot enough to pop!

Carnival Knockdown
Bring the excitement of a carnival home!

Materials:
- several small aluminum carnival or glass bottles
- a soft rubber baseball, or a tightly rolled up pair of old (clean) socks

What You Do:

1. Arrange the glass bottles in a pyramid on soft ground, an area of cut grass, or on top of a sturdy box that's surrounded by soft ground.

2. Stand back about fifteen to twenty feet from your carnival pyramid.

Attempt to knock down all the bottles as you toss your ball toward the glass pyramid!

The Science:

The law of inertia holds the bottles in place. In order to knock them all down, try finding a spot of your pyramid that you can strike that will send all your bottles in motion!

Little Giants

All "grown" up!

Materials:

- a microwave
- a microwave-safe plate full of small, colorful marshmallows

What You Do:

1. Set the microwave for thirty seconds at high power, start it and watch.
2. Remove the little marshmallows, and see the surprise.

Repeat this four more times and write down what you see each time.

The Science:

The first time you remove your little giants, you will notice some marshmallows have expanded larger than others. Repeat the experiment and notice the pattern of puffed-up marshmallows. The microwave heats in a wave-like pattern, which explains why some marshmallows are heated and others that are not in the direct path of the heating waves. But as the plate rotates, the marshmallows are all eventually heated and inflated into little giants. The sugar inside the marshmallows will begin to burn and turn dark brown after several minutes of being exposed to the waves of energy. Continue to heat for several minutes and you should end up with flat, burnt squares of sugar!

Plasma Grapes
Fireball action!

Materials:
- a few grapes, cut in half, yet halves still hinged
- a microwave
- a paper towel

What You Do:

Place the two or three grapes, cut in half yet still with the halves still connected as shown, in the microwave. Turn the microwave on high for about twenty seconds and watch the action!

The Science:

The microwave sends vibrating energy waves, which heat the water, sugar, and skin of the grapes, creating a flow of electricity that ignites into a small plasma fireball!

The Little Bed of Nails

Make the spirits of the ancient Egyptians proud; play it safe with this astonishing scientific demonstration!

Materials and Preparation:
- Have a parent or other adult hammer twenty rows of twenty nails each as straight as possible about an inch apart into a 1-inch-thick piece of solid wood, such as oak or pine. Examine the nails to make sure none are loose.
- Obtain a super large balloon and fill it two-thirds of the way with air.
- Obtain an apple.

Warning: wear heavy metal mesh gloves to protect yourself.

What You Do:

Place your piece of wood so that the nails face up. Toss an apple onto the bed of nails and watch as the fruit becomes impaled.

Now, pressing down evenly from the top, press the balloon against the bed of nails. Finally, press the balloon against only a few nails. Pop!

The Science:

The distribution of nails over a large area of the balloon helps support the oval-shaped balloon. When you toss the apple, its movement, along with the fact that the apple does not get support from as many nails as the balloon did, leads to the piercing of the fruit. If you were to press the balloon against only a few nails, it would not be well supported, causing it to pop!

Alien Smoke Ring Launcher
Send space messages!

Materials and Preparation:

- a strong, round plastic garbage can
- Have an adult cut out a hole 25 centimeters in diameter in the middle of the bottom of the garbage can.
- a large plastic sheet from a major home improvement store
- Get a section to cover and overlap the can's opening by about 5 inches. Fasten it tightly to the can with a bungee cord.
- a smoke bomb, available at various magic or fireworks stores

What you do:

1. Experiment trying to send a blast of air by giving the plastic covering a good whack!

2. Have an adult present to light a smoke ball inside the garbage can. Cover the can with its lid. The smoke will fill the inside of the garbage can.

Now, simply give the plastic a tap and send a "vortex" of smoke rings toward the heavens!

The Science:

Bernoulli's Principle is at work here. A jet of fast-moving air exits the can faster than the surrounding air, creating a vortex. This experiment also demonstrates the fact that air occupies space and has weight, which is made visible by the smoke vortex!

The inspiration for this experiment is Steve Spangler's published experiment, "Giant Smoke Rings," found at www.SteveSpanglerScience.com.

Mad Scientist Hovercraft
Go gliding!

Materials recommended:

- a small, portable leaf blower with a removable front tube
- four wood screws or four metal screws with fender washers and matching nuts
- 6-millimeter-thick plastic sheeting, about 3 1/2 feet in diameter
- duct tape
- a small, round piece of plywood, 1/2 inch thick
- a power drill
- an electric saw
- Use your creativity in building a hovercraft! Below are some suggestions!

Preparation and Experiment:

1. Have an adult cut a four-by-eight foot piece of half-inch-thick plywood in half.

2. Have an adult cut the four-by-four-foot piece of plywood into a three-foot-diameter circle.

3. Sand and tape the edges of the three-foot plywood circle.

4. Measure your leaf blower's air-blowing hole and cut that measurement into your cut plywood circle.

5. Lay the circle on the floor and cut a six-millimeter-thick plastic sheet to size over the board, making it **at least** one inch bigger than the board around the entire circumference.

6. Pull the plastic tight, but not too tight, and have an adult staple it to the hovercraft.

7. Add six two-inch-diameter holes evenly around small wooden disk.

8. Screw small wood pieces with wood or metal screws onto the plastic and wooden circle.

9. Charge your portable leaf blower.

10. Place the fully charged portable leaf blower snuggly into the measured, cut circle from step 4.

Sitting or standing carefully on the top of the disk, have a helper turn on the leaf blower and then help you to begin gliding across the floor or sturdy ground!

Tip: you can find a handyman or carpenter to build for you this hovercraft for less than $100! Be prepared to spend another $150 in supplies, as well!

The Science:

The layer of air provides a cushion as you gently hover across the floor! Air does have weight and takes up space, as illustrated in dramatic form via your homemade hovercraft!